M000112378

# SALMON AND SEA-TROUT FISHERIES OF SCOTLAND

# SALMON AND SEA-TROUT FISHERIES OF SCOTLAND

## An Angler's Guide

Crawford Little

UNWIN HYMAN
LONDON    SYDNEY    WELLINGTON

First published in Great Britain by the Trade Division of Unwin Hyman
Limited, 1990

**UNWIN HYMAN LIMITED**
**15–17 Broadwick Street**
**London W1V 1FP**

Allen & Unwin Australia Pty Ltd
8 Napier Street, North Sydney, NSW 2060, Australia

Allen & Unwin New Zealand Pty with the Port Nicholson Press
Compusales Building, 75 Ghuznee Street, Wellington, New Zealand

---

**British Library Cataloguing in Publication Data**

Little, Crawford
    Salmon and sea-trout fisheries of Scotland.
    1. Great Britain. Freshwater fisheries.
    I. Title
    338.3′727092941

    ISBN 0–04–440487–5

---

Typeset in Bembo by
Nene Phototypesetters Ltd, Northampton
and printed in Great Britain by
The University Press, Cambridge

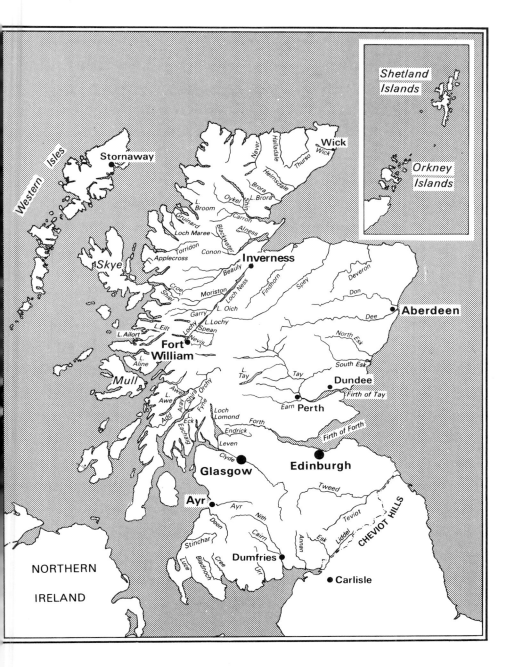

*Salmon and Sea-trout fisheries of Scotland*

# Contents

# Maps

# Introduction
# and Acknowledgements

It is one of those little quirks of the writing craft that the first words of a book are written upon its completion. By that I mean that the Introduction is written *after* the main chapters. This, surely, is only right and proper. You would no more try to introduce a book that you had not yet written than think of writing a 'letter of introduction' to your good friend for a man that you did not know. Well, not quite the same in this case, for I have been lucky enough to fish the salmon and sea-trout fisheries of Scotland, and learned to love them, from a very early age. But, now that I have finished this book, I know them so much better!

I have said that I have fished the rivers and lochs since an early age but, of course, I have not fished them all. It would take almost a lifetime of never visiting the same place twice to gain that knowledge. Even then, the experience would be thin because what can you learn of a fishery and its fish in a month or a week, let alone a day? And this leads me into an acknowledgement of the invaluable help I have been given by so many individuals and organizations, literally too many to mention. Forgive me for not setting out page upon page of your names, but know that my gratitude is, well, as deep as the deepest loch and, without you, this book could never have been completed in its current form.

There are, however, two sides to the coin. I would not mention the fact except that it holds a message for all those who seek their sport in Scotland. Unanswered letters, dismissive telephone calls and the like all point to the fact that, so far as salmon and sea-trout fishing is concerned, we are definitely witnessing a 'sellers' market'. Good fishing is snapped up in the wink of an eye whenever it becomes available. And there are always takers even for waters and times of year which, twenty or thirty years ago, would hardly have seen a wetted line. A number of people, quite rightly in my opinion, requested that their names should not be included; for what would be the point of encouraging false hopes and, let's face it, giving themselves a lot of extra work, where all the fishing has been taken and there is already a twenty year waiting list for the chance that a week, any week, may become available?

Therefore, as one who is also involved in the letting of sport with rod, rifle and gun on the rivers, moors and glens of Scotland, I would end this introduction with a plea for you to complete your reconnaissance of Scottish fisheries within the pages of this and other books. Try to set aside the possibles and probables to arrive at a list of those places where, should fishing be available, you will definitely wish to take it.

Finally, I would mention that the publishers have been kind enough to suggest that this book may evoke sufficient interest to warrant future editions. If any organization or individual would like to contact me via the publishers, I will be very happy to consider any additions or alterations.

As always, tight lines and screaming reels.

The publishers wish to acknowledge the kind permission to use the photographs of Roy Shaw and W. B. Currie.

# 1 The Solway Firth

## BORDER ESK

The Border Esk is the first river encountered on moving up the west coast from England into Scotland. Indeed, its mouth and lower stretches are in England. All the middle and upper stretches, however, as well as its major tributaries, are in Scotland. Uppermost of these tributaries are the White Esk and the Black Esk. It is after their meeting, just to the south of Castle O'er, that the Border Esk is formed. Between Castle O'er and Langholm, the major town situated on the river, it is joined by a number of other tributaries, the principal of which are the Meggat Water, the Ewes and the Wauchope. Just south of Langholm the Esk is joined by the Tarras and then, beyond the village of Canonbie, the river is joined by the Liddle, its major tributary, and a salmon and sea-trout fishery of much importance. The Border Esk enters England upstream of Longtown and flows on to empty into the Solway Firth.

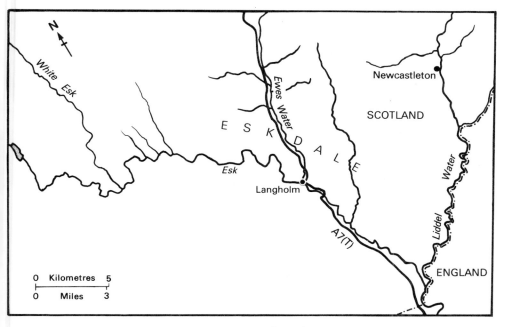

Map 1    *Border Esk*

## Season

*Salmon*   1 February to 31 October (best September–October)
*Sea-trout*   1 May to 30 September (best June–August).

## Fish

Border Esk has its runs of late-season salmon, but it is as a renowned sea-trout fishery that it is known both near and far. Sea-trout sport in the summer dusks and dawns can be truly spectacular. Most of the river is controlled by the Esk and Liddle Fishery Association. Anglers on the association stretches recorded a combined total of very nearly 4,500 sea-trout in the season of 1988, with some local rods scoring their century. In the same season, the association's water on the Lower Liddle produced more than 700 sea-trout.

Equally, the association's water on the Esk produced over 500 salmon in 1988, with roughly 400 of these taken in the last two months of the season, and 40 from the Lower Liddle. And so, far famed as it is as a sea-trout fishery, surely, with catches in excess of 400 packed into two short autumn months, the Border Esk must also be seen as a very good salmon river.

## Fishing

Border Esk sea-trout respond well to the traditional dusk-to-dawn night-fishing approach. Most pools are not so deep or so slow as to require a concerted effort with sinking lines and large lures, though an intermediate or sink-tip can work well once the initial fast activity of the dusk rise has passed. Some pools offer relatively straightforward, easy wading but others do not, and a thorough reconnaissance is recommended before night fishing. Much of the river, between Langholm and Canonbie, is tree-lined, and the ability to Spey- or steeple-cast can often prove a useful asset.

In times of high water during the summer sea-trout months, worm and spinner can produce good baskets of fish. In the interests of conservation, however, and to protect the future of their own sport, anglers are advised not to take large numbers of herling, the young sea-trout. The fly can also work very well in daylight conditions of high water, particularly as the river begins to clear and fall.

## Tackle

*Sea-trout*

A number of experienced local sea-trout fishermen stick with their double-handed rods of 12 feet for sea-trout fishing with the fly. However, the majority feel that there is greater sport and enjoyment to be found in the use of more sensitive single-handed carbon rods in the 10–11 foot range, rated AFTM 7. A floating line will see the fisherman through the dusk rise, after which he may care to try an intermediate or sink-tip.

Sea-trout fishing has experienced an explosion in the number of patterns of flies used. It seems that there is virtually a different favourite for each and every fisherman. However, the Border Esk, like so many sea-trout rivers, proves the common-sense approach which states that when the sea-trout are taking, the long-established traditional patterns will work as well as anything. Local favourites include the Whaup and Yellow and Whaup and Silver, otherwise known as the Langholm Silver. However, now that the whaup (curlew) is a protected species, these flies are becoming difficult to obtain. One very good and experienced local fisherman tells me that he has used a Teal, Blue and Silver on the point and a Black Pennell on the dropper for virtually all his fishing life. Other favourites would include the Peter Ross, the Silver March Brown and the Invicta. Many locals swear by a Greenwell's Spider tied on a size 10 or 12 bronze double for when the water is low and the fish are wary.

*Salmon*

Border Esk is far from being a large river. Therefore, most salmon fishermen find that the water can be covered adequately with a double-handed carbon rod of 13 or 14 feet, which allows delicate presentation and accuracy when required. Spey casting can be a great advantage when faced with high banks and trees. Esk salmon do not require such large sizes of fly as we would associate, say, with the Tweed. Blue Charm and the Silver Doctor can both work well, as can the Garry Dog. Autumn salmon in September and October often respond well to a fly containing red and yellow in its make-up, hence the popularity of the Garry. If the angler intends to fish fly regardless of water height and colour, he should also carry some 2-inch Garry Dog or Yellow and Orange tube flies.

*Spinning for Salmon*

Having mentioned flies for use in high, coloured water, I must say that, faced with these conditions, most Esk salmon fishermen will resort to the worm or spinner. A spinning rod of 8–9 feet with a fixed-spool reel loaded with 12–15 lb bs nylon provides a good Esk spinning outfit. Brown-and-gold or black-and-gold Devon minnows can work well, as do the Yellow Belly and Copper Toby in the late-season months.

## Access

Tickets and a brochure for the association water are available from

> The Secretary
> Esk and Liddle Fisheries Association
> Bank of Scotland Buildings
> Langholm
> Dumfriesshire
> *Telephone* 03873 80428

## ANNAN

The Annan rises in the Moffat Hills in Dumfriesshire and flows for some 40 miles before entering the Solway Firth downstream of the town of Annan, by which stage it has become a river of some size. The main headwater is the Elvan, originating close to Leadhills, though the source of the river is recognized as Loch Skeen at the top of the Grey Mare's Tail waterfall.

The nature of the Annan – compared, say, with a typically Highland stream – is rather towards the sluggish. Not all of the water, you understand. In some sections the river flows quite quickly. However, the overall slow nature of the big pools is something that must be allowed for, and it will be discussed in the section on fishing.

The Annan, like all the Solway rivers, is a spate river. In other words, it is heavily dependent on rainfall to raise water levels, bring in fresh fish, and improve the fishing chances. There is nothing sluggish about a big spate on the Annan. Forestry drainage in its catchment area leads inevitably to a fast run-off. The river rises fast and to the colour of potter's clay. It can take a day or two to clear and for fishing to improve.

## Season

*Salmon and Sea-trout* 25 February to 15 November (best September–November for salmon, June–July for sea-trout).

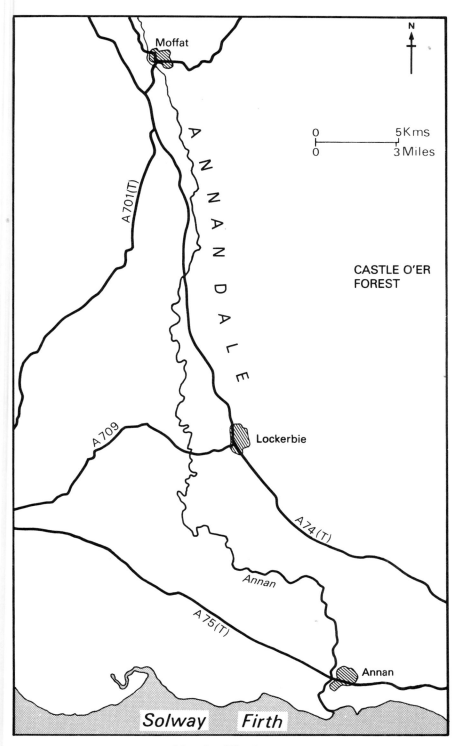

Map 2    *The Annan*

## Fish

The Annan has enjoyed a long reputation for producing salmon throughout the fishing season. However, like most rivers, the Annan has times of woe as well as joy and, at the present time, the spring run is certainly suffering. Time was when this river could be depended upon to produce quantities of salmon in February. Nowadays, the runs are but a fraction of those of the past and those fish that are taken are usually lying downstream of Milnbie. It is very sad to remember the days when a hundred or more prime springers would be grassed in the opening weeks of the season, and as many as twenty or thirty on the opening day.

The summer months, on spate rivers everywhere, are totally dependent on rainfall, which, despite what non-fishing visitors to Scotland may say, is seldom if ever enough to please those eagerly awaiting the arrival of summer salmon and grilse. But then comes a truly wet summer, and the Annan beats can provide great sport.

Also in the summer, sea-trout fishing on the Annan can be excellent. The average weight of these sea-trout is good at around 2 lb and every season shows a smattering of big fish in the 5–8 lb category.

It is for autumn salmon, however, as on most Solway rivers, that the Annan's reputation rests, with numbers steadily increasing after the end of August. It is not just quantity that the Annan is noted for at this time. The river's autumn fish run big as well, with an average weight of more than 12 lb. Each season Annan proves that it can produce specimen salmon in the 20 and 30 lb classes.

## Fishing

It has been stated that Annan is a spate river; it has also been said that its spates can run high and dirty. This is the reason, perhaps, why worm and spinner are the traditionally favoured techniques. A number of beats, however, do impose a fly-only rule. In the modern age, when more and more fishermen are becoming fly purists and would prefer not to have to fish a pool alongside wormers and spinners, this can be viewed as a shrewd as well as a sporting stand to take.

What makes this fly-only rule work well is that it tends to be found on those beats that have good, streamy water particularly suited to fishing the fly across without the fisherman's intervention. Of course, where required in rather slower stretches, the fly can be made to swim attractively by gentle handlining. This can be very productive in some of the big, slow pools – much more so than backing up, I have found, though why this should be I really cannot say. Backing up just does not seem to travel very well from its Highland home to the Solway rivers.

*Tackle*
The same tackle and flies as described for the Border Esk can be used on the Annan, except that since the river is that little bit bigger and wider many Annan fly fishermen prefer the extra casting and handling range of a 15-foot rod when after salmon, certainly on the middle and lower stretches.

In addition to the spinners mentioned for the Esk, many Annan spinners swear by an all-red Devon minnow for provoking autumn salmon to take.

**Access**

Access to the Annan is excellent virtually throughout its length, except for the Newby and Distillery beats just upstream of Annan, which have now been timeshared. However, not all the shares have been let and fishing may be available. Contact:

Water Bailiff
Newbie Mill Cottage
Violet Bank
Annan
*Telephone* 04612 2608

The next beat upstream is the well-known Hoddom Water, which, in addition to daily tickets, offers evening sea-trout fishing permits during the summer months. Contact:

Mrs Ward
Ecclefechan Hotel
Ecclefechan
*Telephone* 05763 488

Castle Milk Estate has 2½ miles of fly-only fishing not far south of Lockerbie, for which they issue daily and weekly tickets. Contact:

The Factor
Castle Milk Estates Office
Norwood
Lockerbie
*Telephone* 05762 203

The Royal Four Towns stretch is 2 miles of what looks like rather uninspiring sluggish water situated between Lockerbie and Lochmaben. However, it offers easy wading and fishing for novice anglers. Sea-trout are present in quantity in a normal summer, and the stretch can hold a good stock of salmon in the autumn. I do not think that it is unfair to suggest that this stretch is of more interest to the spinner than it might be to the fly fisherman. Contact the Castle Milk Estates office (as above) or:

> Mrs Radcliff
> Jay-Ar
> Preston House Road
> Hightae
> Lockerbie
> *Telephone* 0387 810 220

Halleaths and Dryfeholm lie upstream of the Royal Four Towns and are both fly-only. Halleaths is let on a weekly and season basis and Dryfeholm is season only, Halleaths being on the right bank and Dryfeholm on the left. While these are generally fly-only waters, it should be noted that worm is allowed during times of flood, but only between 15 March and 30 September. Contact:

> McJerrow & Stevenson, Solicitors
> 55 High Street
> Lockerbie
> *Telephone* 05762 2123

The Upper-Annandale Angling Association has two stretches on the main river as well as some tributary water. Its topmost stretch offers 4½ miles of the Annan just below the town of Moffat, and one mile on the Moffat Water. Below their upper Annan stretch is the Annandale Estates beat, and then the association has another 4-mile stretch of the Annan, as well as tributary water on the Kinnel and Dryfe. Worm is allowed from 1 May, regardless of water conditions. Before 30 September spinning is allowed only when bridge markers are covered, but after that date it is allowed irrespective of water conditions. These upper stretches are not likely to show much sport until well into September but then, given a running height of water in the Annan, the sport can come fast and furious. Sea-trout, on the other hand, are well up to this part of the river in midsummer, and show a preference for the smaller sizes of traditional sea-trout flies. Wee doubles and spider patterns can be deadly in the dusk. Incidentally, there is no Saturday fishing for visitors. For tickets contact:

> Beattock House Hotel
> *Telephone* 06833 402

'Clickety Click'
65 High Street
Lockerbie
*Telephone* 05762 2400

J. Black
1 Rosehill
Grange Road
Moffat
*Telephone* 0683 20104

Annandale Estates beat is an attractive and easily accessible stretch, close to the A74 road from Carlisle to Glasgow and Edinburgh. Day tickets are available up to 15 September and weekly tickets throughout the season. Contact:

Annandale Estates Fishing
*Telephone* 05764 317

## NITH

From its source near Dalmellington in Ayrshire, the Nith soon flows into northern Dumfriesshire at Kirkconnel and on past the main fishing centres of Sanquhar, Thornhill and Dumfries before emptying into the Solway Firth. Its length is approximately 50 miles.

The Nith is almost canal-like above Sanquhar, with long stretches of very sluggish water. From Sanquhar down, however, although there is no white water except in the Drumlanrig Gorge just north of Thornhill in times of high water, the river flows majestically through excellent holding pools.

Much of upper Nithsdale has been subjected to extensive forestry plantings with their associated drainage schemes. This means that the Nith will rise and fall far quicker than in previous times. This factor, allied to rich agricultural land in the middle and lower sections, result in fast and dirty spates, running bank high and the colour of potter's clay.

## Season

25 February to 30 November (best September–November for salmon, June–July for sea-trout).

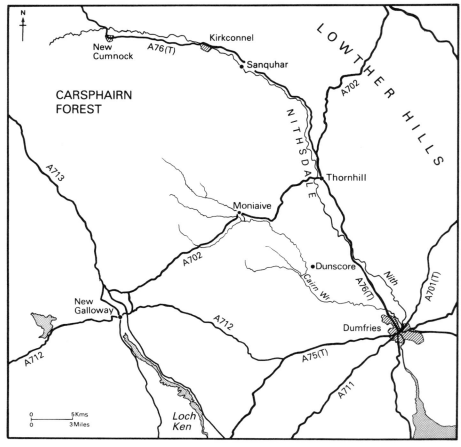

Map 3    *The Nith*

**Fish**

*Salmon*

This is one of the few rivers that can boast an average rod catch of over 3,000 salmon and grilse each season, and it continues to improve.

The Nith is recognised as one of the outstanding autumn salmon rivers, with the vast bulk of the catch being taken from September until the end of November. The river is also capable of producing good numbers of summer salmon and grilse in wet seasons. Spring is less generous but an average of 50 salmon are caught for each of the months of March, April and May. Most of these springers are taken below the Cauld (weir) in Dumfries. Fish will not ascend this obstruction until the water temperature exceeds 42°F.

The average weight of salmon caught on the Nith is about 9 lb. However, each season produces larger fish, a good number over 20 lb.

### Sea-trout

The Nith is also a noted sea-trout river. Sport with these fish normally gets under way in late May and continues through into the start of September. June, July and August are the most productive months.

The average weight of Nith sea-trout is a little over 2 lb and it is not rare to take fish of over 5 lb.

## Fishing

The Nith is a spate river, with catches of migratory fish being heavily dependent upon rainfall.

After heavy rain, the river runs high and coloured and, inevitably, it will be the second or third day of the spate before serious fishing can begin, worm normally being the most productive method. On the following day, with the water still falling and clearing, salmon will be caught on the spinner, and the fly becomes productive. A few days after this the river will be back to normal level and catches begin to fade.

### Tackle and Techniques

Individual tastes differ but due to the character of the Nith fishings fishermen might be well advised to equip themselves with fly, spinning and worming tackle.

The river is of medium size, and most fishermen find that they can cover practically all the pools adequately when wearing only thigh waders.

### Fly Fishing for Salmon

Most fishermen use double-handed carbon fly rods of 13–15 feet on this river, though a single-handed rod of about 10 feet can be used for summer salmon and grilse.

Favoured salmon flies include the Stoat's Tail, Hairy Mary, Yellow Dog, Blue Charm, Shrimp Fly and, traditionally the most favoured of all, the Brown Turkey. Local fishermen tend to stick with the spinner while the river is high, therefore the standard size of fly is about a 6. Those who fish the fly in high water find that a 2-inch Yellow Dog tube fly can be very successful.

*The salmon angler's prize – a perfect 8 lb hen fish*

## Spinning

A spinning rod of 9 feet and a fixed-spool reel loaded with 12–15-lb bs nylon is the basic salmon spinning outfit for the Nith.

Most salmon are caught on 2–3-inch Devon Minnows, favoured colours being black-and-gold, brown-and-gold, black-and-red, black-and-orange, green-and-yellow (Yellow Belly) and the blue-and-pearl plastic Devon produced by Gordon Griffiths Tackle. Toby spoons in medium sizes also work well, particularly during high water in those pools with a fairly strong current.

## Worm Fishing

The humble worm accounts for a significant proportion of Nith salmon caught by locals. Many use the same rod, reel and line as for spinning. However, a few local traditionalists use the fly rod and carry a fly reel loaded with nylon monofilament.

A bunch of lobworms is cast across and upstream of the fisherman. Just enough weight is attached a few feet above the baited hook to ensure that the worms come trundling back slowly on the bed of the river. Eventually the worms trundle inshore and downstream of the fisherman, who then waits for a few moments to give a hesitant fish a chance to pick the worms up. After a few nods and tugs the salmon moves off steadily and the strike is made. Otherwise, if no fish has followed the bunch of worms, the fisherman takes a step and lobs the worms out again, across and upstream.

No great length of line is required; many experts in this method practically fish the worm under the rod tip, because salmon lie close in to the bank, out of the full force of the high water.

Worm fishing is normally allowed only during times of high water.

*Fishing for Sea-trout*

Nith sea-trout can be taken on worm and spinner, probably a Mepps or small Toby spoon, in high water. However, the most popular method after the water levels have fallen is the fly.

Fishermen who know the Nith and its sea-trout tend towards fairly small sizes of traditional patterns, size 8 or 10 for night work. A useful selection of patterns would include Peter Ross, Teal, Blue and Silver, Greenwell's Glory, Black Pennell and Wickham's Fancy. Normally two flies are fished on the leader as Nith sea-trout, like those of many Scottish rivers, can respond well to a bushy dropper such as the Pennell.

During the hours of daylight, particularly in the evening and early morning, before dusk and after dawn, sea-trout on the Nith may be tempted by a team of spider patterns tied on 12 and 14 hooks, cast over runs and streams beneath the shade of a high bank and trees. In order to be successful, the fisherman must really stalk his quarry and fish 'fine and far off'. An alternative method at this time is short–lining, scuttering a bushy bob fly over the faster runs. Again, slow movements and careful wading are essential.

## Access

Nithsdale District Council controls 2 miles of excellent water in, and on either side of, Dumfries. Fishing pressure and the number of anglers can be intense, but little wonder! This relatively short stretch leading into the estuary produced approximately 1,800 salmon and grilse and 1,000 sea-trout in the season of 1988. Daily, weekly and seasonal tickets are available. Monday to Friday only for visitors. Contact:

Nithsdale District Council
Buccleuch Street
Dumfries
*Telephone* 0387 53166

Travelling upstream from Dumfries, the fisherman finds himself on the Dumfries and Galloway Angling Association's stretch, 2 miles of the Nith at Carnsalloch. Fly and worm are the rule, except when the markers are covered, when spinning and shrimp are permitted. Daily and weekly tickets are available, but no Saturday fishing for visitors. Contact:

J. McMillan
Tackle Shop
6 Friar's Vennel
Dumfries
*Telephone* 0387 52075

Upstream of the D&GAA stretch are a number of private beats. Some of these are virtually a closed shop so far as access is concerned. However, inquiries might be made to:

Smiths Gore
Chartered Surveyors
Castle Street
Dumfries

Upstream of Auldgirth, Barjarg Estate lets nearly 2 miles of excellent single-bank fishing, which can include self-catering accommodation. This water offers good summer sea-trout and autumn salmon fishing for individuals and small parties. Contact:

Andrew Hunter-Arundel
Newhall
Barjarg Estate
Auldgirth
Dumfries
*Telephone* 0848 31342

The opposite bank to Barjarg is the Closeburn Castle timeshare beat. Occasional vacancies and cancellations may make fishing available on a weekly basis. These are usually notified to:

Trigony House Hotel
Closeburn
Thornhill
Dumfriesshire
*Telephone* 0848 31211

Above Barjarg and Closeburn is the excellent and deservedly popular Mid-Nithsdale Angling Association stretch. In 1988, Mid-Nithsdale reported 525 salmon and 587 sea-trout. It is a 3-mile stretch containing seventeen named pools. Worm and spinning are allowed only in high water, fly at any time – from size 10 in low-water summer conditions up to 2½-inch Waddingtons and tubes towards season's close. No day permits on Saturdays or during November, but a 3-day as well as a weekly permit is available in that month. Demand is such that you are strongly advised to book your fishing if planning a visit from September onwards. Contact:

I. R. Milligan
123 Drumlanrig Street
Thornhill
Dumfriesshire
*Telephone* 0848 30555

Above the Bridge at Thornhill is the start of the Buccleuch Estates beats. Demand is high but fishing may sometimes be available. There are three main beats, Upper, Middle and Lower, with a subsidiary beat, the Nith Linns, being highest of all and set in the Drumlanrig Gorge. The Linns can offer good but challenging and rather difficult fishing. Each of the beats takes two guests, and it is possible for a third rod to fish for a fairly small supplementary charge. Contact:

Buccleuch Estates
Marrburn
Thornhill
Dumfriesshire
*Telephone* 08486 283

Upstream of the Buccleuch waters there are nine miles of Nith fishings, stretching up to the town of Sanquhar, which are con-trolled by the Upper-Nithsdale Angling Club. This stretch will produce well in excess of 1,000 sea-trout in a normal season, and perhaps 500 salmon and grilse in the back-end months. Contact:

W. Forsyth, Solicitor
Secretary
Upper-Nithsdale Angling Club
100 High Street
Sanquhar
Dumfriesshire
*Telephone* 0659 50241

## Catch Statistics

### ROD CATCHES ON RIVER NITH OVER TEN YEARS

| Year | Salmon | Grilse | Sea-trout | Total Migratory |
|------|--------|--------|-----------|-----------------|
| 1976 | 750 | 308 | 4,816 | 5,874 |
| 1977 | 1,020 | 316 | 3,451 | 4,787 |
| 1978 | 968 | 367 | 3,426 | 4,761 |
| 1979 | 1,072 | 608 | 3,896 | 5,576 |
| 1980 | 1,110 | 777 | 5,419 | 7,306 |
| 1981 | 1,273 | 350 | 6,218 | 7,841 |
| 1982 | 1,178 | 625 | 4,997 | 6,800 |
| 1983 | 1,238 | 450 | 4,612 | 6,300 |
| 1984 | 1,633 | 664 | 2,456 | 4,753 |
| 1985 | 1,520 | 480 | 4,125 | 6,125 |

*Notes*

Best year of recent decades was 1964: 2,611 salmon, 637 grilse and 8,256 sea-trout – a total of 11,504 migratory fish.

Ulcerative dermal necrosis, the salmon disease, broke out on the Nith in 1967. Catches were immediately halved. It has taken the river nearly twenty years to recover to something approaching its former glories. The season of 1987 closely rivalled that of 1964.

Smaller catches of salmon during 1976 and 1978 are generally attributed to drought conditions.

## Seasonal Variations – Best Times

The following figures are the reported catches from the Buccleuch Estates beats at Drumlanrig Castle, Thornhill. They can be taken as showing the general monthly pattern of sport on the Nith.

### BUCCLEUCH ESTATES – MIDDLE NITH

#### Salmon

| | 1976 | 1977 | 1978 | 1979 | 1980 | 1981 | 1982 | 1983 | 1984 | 1985 | 1986 | 1987 | 1988 |
|------|------|------|------|------|------|------|------|------|------|------|------|------|------|
| March | — | — | 1 | — | — | — | — | — | — | — | — | — | — |
| April | 1 | 1 | 1 | 2 | 4 | 2 | 1 | 1 | — | 1 | — | 1 | — |
| May | 2 | 4 | — | 3 | — | 4 | 1 | 2 | — | 2 | 2 | — | 1 |
| June | 1 | 3 | 1 | 2 | 9 | 10 | 2 | — | — | 7 | 12 | 1 | 3 |
| July | 3 | 1 | 6 | 6 | 20 | 16 | 3 | — | — | 3 | 20 | 12 | 31 |
| August | 4 | 3 | 5 | 24 | 51 | 15 | 34 | 2 | — | 42 | 64 | 27 | 69 |
| Sept. | 16 | 13 | 15 | 36 | 43 | 13 | 21 | 22 | 21 | 53 | 27 | 45 | 66 |

| . | 21 | 23 | 10 | 11 | 32 | 37 | 52 | 49 | 70 | 57 | 8 | 38 | 73 |
|---|----|----|----|----|----|----|----|----|----|----|----|----|----|
| v. | 13 | 11 | 5 | 16 | 14 | 13 | 16 | 29 | 81 | 40 | 48 | 40 | 85 |
| TALS | 61 | 59 | 44 | 100 | 173 | 110 | 130 | 105 | 172 | 205 | 181 | 164 | 328 |

*es*

dependence of the Nith fishing upon late-summer and autumn salmon is obvious, and
.ires no further amplification.
'he effect of drought conditions on the summers of 1983 and 1984 are clearly shown, and
nlight the fact that the Nith is a spate-dependent river. Given a wet August, as in 1980,
5, 1986 and again in 1988, however, salmon and sport can come fast and furious.
'aken over a lengthy period, October has consistently proved the best month for salmon
he middle Nith.

## BUCCLEUCH ESTATES – MIDDLE NITH

### Sea-trout

| | 1976 | 1977 | 1978 | 1979 | 1980 | 1981 | 1982 | 1983 | 1984 | 1985 | 1986 | 1987 | 1988 |
|---|------|------|------|------|------|------|------|------|------|------|------|------|------|
| ·il | 2 | 1 | 2 | — | — | — | — | 2 | — | — | — | 2 | 1 |
| y | 39 | 9 | 2 | 10 | 8 | 18 | 4 | 26 | 2 | 9 | 3 | 10 | 4 |
| e | 85 | 25 | 34 | 78 | 142 | 94 | 36 | 82 | 16 | 74 | 45 | 51 | 54 |
| , | 80 | 30 | 38 | 73 | 78 | 130 | 81 | 61 | 28 | 86 | 54 | 46 | 117 |
| gust | 53 | 44 | 32 | 57 | 66 | 72 | 75 | 19 | 22 | 59 | 49 | 23 | 57 |
| t. | 68 | 63 | 31 | 16 | 32 | 30 | 24 | 56 | 19 | 12 | 8 | 13 | 13 |
| :. | 4 | 6 | 5 | 3 | 3 | — | — | 2 | 3 | — | 2 | 2 | 3 |
| v. | 5 | 1 | 1 | 3 | 1 | 6 | 3 | 1 | 3 | 5 | 1 | — | 2 |
| TALS | 336 | 179 | 145 | 240 | 330 | 350 | 225 | 249 | 93 | 245 | 160 | 147 | 251 |

*es*

relatively low catch of sea-trout in 1984 can be seen alongside salmon catches for the
ıe year, with no salmon taken until into September. While sea-trout are not nearly so
te-dependent as salmon, they still need some water in order to run the river.
'he Nith has been described as a 'late' sea-trout river by some authorities but, as the
ve figures show, this should not be taken to mean that they start to run late but rather
:, after an often early start, they continue over the best months of July to September
.ough, by the end of September at least, the fish will usually have become stale and
›ured. Those taken after that date tend to be hooked unintentionally by fishermen in
suit of salmon.

# CAIRN

The Cairn is the major tributary of the Nith. It flows past the
villages of Moniaive, Dunscore and Newtonairds to join the Nith
close to Newbridge, just north of Dumfries. It is a small river, and
much overgrown with trees, but with deep and often productive
pools.

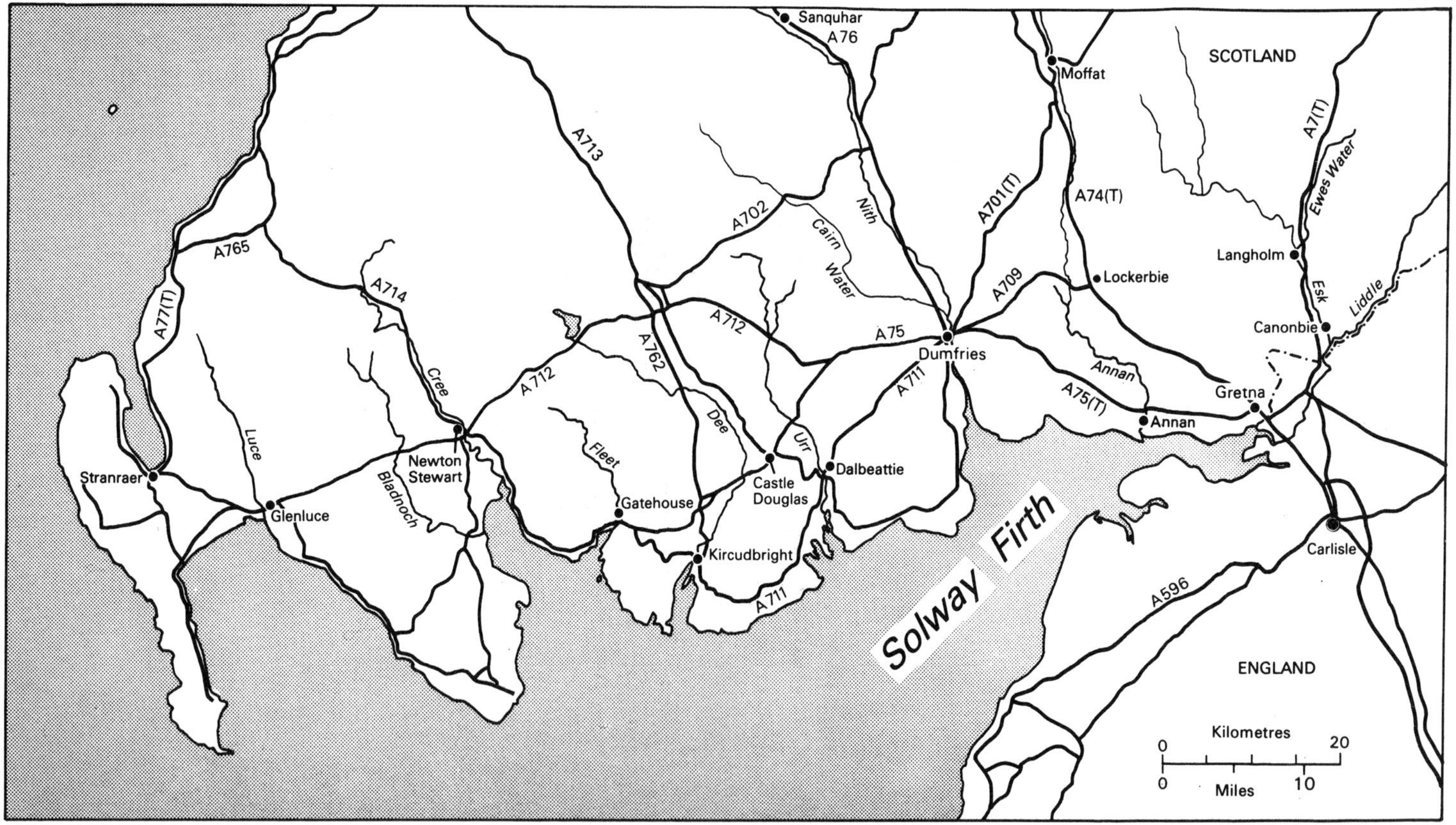

Map 4   *The Solway Rivers*

## Fishing and Seasons

Fishing on the Cairn is very similar to that on the Nith, only on a very much smaller scale. Its season is variable for salmon and sea-trout, being from 25 February to 31 October on the lower stretches, and from 1 April to 31 October on the rest. Most of the river is fly-only until 1 May. However, just to confuse the issue, one stretch is fished until 30 November!

Sea-trout, summer-salmon and grilse fishing, given good water height, can be very good, but most salmon are taken in September and October.

The Cairn fishes well after a spate, but it can be found that the taking time is relatively short-lived. It is an intimate little river where catches can depend heavily on being in just the right place at the right time. Also, because of the heavily treed nature of its banks and those deep, streamy pools, it is a stream that fishes particularly well with the worm, although fly can be used on some more open stretches. Catch the Cairn in a productive mood and it can be very generous.

## Access

Dumfries and Galloway Angling Association controls most of the Cairn, but the Nithsdale Council ticket (see Nith) includes a productive stretch at the joining of the two rivers. Contact addresses and telephone numbers are given under the Nith, above.

There is a short but productive stretch of water at Cluden Rocks, which is where you can fish up to 30 November. Day tickets are sold. Contact:

> J. Howie
> West Cluden Farm
> Irongray
> Dumfries
> *Telephone* 0387 720314

## URR

As we travel out of Dumfriesshire and into Galloway, the first salmon and sea-trout river of any consequence is the Urr. For its apparent small size it has a fairly large catchment area and flows for 30 miles from its source at Loch Urr to the sea at Kippford. It also shows quite contrasting characteristics, being moorland in its upper stretches but then fairly sluggish as it flows through the richer agricultural ground of the coastlands. Agriculture, combined with forestry drainage operations, has affected the nature of the Urr. It has always been a spate stream, but now the rise and fall of its spates are far more rapid than in previous times.

## Season

25 February to 30 November (best September–November).

## Fishing

It is a shame that drainage schemes have so sorely affected the Urr, as they have so many rivers. And yet, catch the river at a good time, with a nice height of water to set fish on the move, and it will show brief bursts of good sport.

Surprisingly, perhaps, when compared with other Solway rivers, the Urr is hardly worth mentioning as a sea-trout river. Equally, while some summer salmon and grilse may be taken, this is very heavily dependent on unseasonally high rainfall. It is in the back end that Urr can show its best sport.

Most modern hairwing patterns of fly can work well, as well as shrimp patterns, but many experienced local rods stick with traditional favourites such as the Jock Scott, the Brown Turkey and the Black Doctor.

Because of the nature of the river, however, most of the Urr's salmon fall either to worm or to spinner. In this small river spinners should be not too large. Devon minnows of about 1½ inches are useful, as well as the smaller sizes of copper Toby spoons.

Fly fishing can be carried out with a single-handed rod of 10–11 feet, or a double-handed of 12–13 feet, while an 8-foot spinning rod will cover the river quite admirably. Remember, this is not a big river and casting accuracy is far more important than range.

Dalbeattie Anging Association has the lower 3½ miles of the Urr, then another stretch of 1 mile below the Castle Douglas Angling Association's water. For daily and weekly tickets for either of these associations' waters contact:

M. McCowan
Tackle Shop
43 High Street
Dalbeattie
*Telephone* 0556 610270

Tommy's Sports
174 King Street
Castle Douglas
*Telephone* 0556 2851

## KIRKUDBRIGHTSHIRE DEE

The Kirkudbridghtshire Dee could be said to be a river whose game fish have been sacrificed in order to meet the energy needs of man. When the river was harnessed for the generation of hydro-electricity, water levels were raised and about half the river's spawning potential was lost. Then there were problems with the fish pass. Just when these were thought to have been put right, UDN (ulcerative dermal necrosis) hit hard. Things are certainly improving now in terms of migratory fish stocks but, even so, the fish are notoriously dour to take.

Much of the river is deep and very sluggish. This holds little attraction for salmon, but is a natural harbour for pike and perch, which prey on immature salmon. Indeed, there are many fishermen who would suggest that the Dee should be regarded as a primarily coarse fishery, with some good trout fishing, but not worthy of any major consideration in terms of migratory fish and their pursuit. Nevertheless, both salmon in the back end and sea-trout in the summer are caught.

### Season

11 February to 31 October.

### Access

The Balmaghie beat has two miles of double-bank fishing down to Threave Castle, close to Castle Douglas. For details telephone 055 667249.

## FLEET

A delightfully picturesque little river, flowing past Gatehouse, the Fleet properly goes by that name only up to four miles above Gatehouse, where it is formed by the joining of the Big Water of Fleet and the Little Water of Fleet, which both rise in the Galloway hills. These rivers flow for much of their length through woodland.

Below Gatehouse, the Fleet itself becomes sluggish and less attractive to the fisherman.

## Season

1 June to 31 October (best August–October for salmon, June–August for sea-trout).

## Fish

The waters that join to create the Fleet system cannot be regarded as wildly productive, and it should be regarded as a sea-trout rather than a salmon fishery. Despite efforts made, such as stocking with 10,000 sea-trout ova in 1984, this river suffers the scourge of acidity as a result of acid rain, and until national and international pollution of this kind becomes a thing of the past there seems to be little that can be done at a local level. The season of 1988 might be viewed as fairly typical, producing 20 salmon with an average weight of 8½ lb, 4 grilse averaging 6 lb, and 135 sea-trout averaging 1¼ lb.

## Fishing

To try to catch a salmon on the Fleet you might choose a Hairy Mary or a Silver Doctor. The size need not be large, say a size 8 when the river has settled. A double-handed rod of 12 feet is prefectly adequate, or a single-handed rod of about 10 feet, which will also serve for sea-trout. Flies for sea-trout are generally used in size 10 for night work. Traditional patterns are the thing, such as the Butcher, the Coachman and the Teal, Blue and Silver.

Spinning is allowed only when the line on the marker posts is covered. Try a 1½-inch Devon minnow, a small Toby or a Mepps spoon.

## Access

Virtually the entire Fleet system is owned by the Cally Estates, who let their three beats – the Lower, Middle and Upper Stretches – to the public. They also have a stretch on the Little Water of Fleet for sea-trout. Contact:

> Murray Arms Hotel
> Gatehouse of Fleet
> Dumfries and Galloway
> *Telephone* 05574 207

## CREE

From its source in Loch Moan, the Cree has an extensive catchment area. It has a number of steep, rocky tributaries in the Ayrshire and Kirkudbrightshire hills which create fast rises in spate conditions. This characteristic can be likened to rain falling on a slate roof compared with one of thatch.

The river and tributaries lose their thin hill-stream nature below the falls above Birch Linn, some miles upstream from Bargrennan. Below the falls there is a series of deep pools. As you would expect, salmon congregate in this area on their upstream migration until water conditions are right to run the falls and on to the upstream spawning redds. Farther downstream the river becomes somewhat sluggish, but there are still some very productive pools in the Penninghame area. Indeed, from Penninghame down to Linloskin, a short distance above Newton Stewart, the river regains its momentum, and from here down to the salt it looks good fly-fishing water. Incidentally, it seems that sea-trout seldom ascend higher than Linloskin.

### Season

1 March to 14 October (best March–April and September–October for salmon, June–July for sea-trout).

### Fish

Those sea-trout that run up to Linloskin, seeking to enter the numerous tributaries and burns that enter the main river in its lower section, do so mainly in June and July.

Turning to salmon, it is interesting to discover that the Cree, besides the Annan, is one of the few Solway rivers that can show salmon sport from March onwards. Numbers build up if water conditions are suitable for summer salmon and grilse to run and then, slotting back into the true Solway character, sport peaks in the back-end months of September and October.

### Fishing

A great deal of the lower Cree is well suited to fly fishing. Even where the pools verge on the sluggish there is no real problem, since they can be fished effectively by handlining the fly to give it life and action. One of the many patterns of Shrimp Fly can work well, or you might fish the traditional favourites – Black Doctor, Blue Charm or Hairy Mary. As on many autumn rivers, a fly with gold and orange in its make-up, such as the Goldie or the Dunkeld, can prove effective. A 12- or 13-foot rod might be adequate for low-water summer conditions, but there would be no harm in looking for greater power and length, particularly in times of high water or with sinking line.

Of course you might choose to spin with a 9-foot rod and fixed-spool reel, using a blue-and-silver or a blue-and-pearl Devon minnow in spring, or a brown-and-gold one later on. And a bunch of lobworms will take its share of the Cree's salmon.

For sea-trout in the lower stretches, worm or spinner – perhaps a small silver Mepps – can work in daylight, given high water, and then the traditional team of wet flies as the water starts to fall and clear. With the river falling farther the night fisherman comes into his own, with stand-bys such as the Peter Ross, the Teal, Blue and Silver, the Black Pennell, the White Moth and so on working well. Streamer flies – which may be taken for sandeels by the sea-trout when they are fresh off the tide – can be deadly at times.

## Access

A good selection of Cree salmon and sea-trout fishing is available to the public. Newton Stewart and District Angling Association has almost 2 miles of fishing at Newton Stewart, which produced about 200 salmon and grilse in 1988. No visitors on Saturdays, no bait until after 16 April, spinning and worm thereafter only when the markers are covered. The permit also allows fishing on certain tributaries, and the association also has the fishing on certain trout lochs, if the migratory fish are not co-operating. Contact:

> Galloway Guns and Tackle
> Newton Stewart
> Dumfries and Galloway
> *Telephone* 0671 3404

> D. G. Guns & Tackle
> Albert Street
> Newton Stewart
> Dumfries and Galloway
> *Telephone* 0671 3224

Galloway Estate water produced about 400 salmon in 1988 from its five miles of double-bank fishing. It has three beats with 18 pools, and a gillie is included. A 'price guarantee' system operates for those wishing to take a beat for three years. Contact:

Mrs J. Robb
G. M. Thomson & Co
Victoria Street
Newton Stewart
Dumfries and Galloway
*Telephone* 0671 2887

## BLADNOCH

This Galloway river has its source in Loch Maberry and runs about 20 miles to salt water in the Solway Firth. In this short distance the Bladnoch presents an ever-changing picture. In its upper section, from the loch down to Glassoch, there are good, deep holding pools and gravelly runs. This contrasts sharply with the stretch from Glassoch down to Barhosie Dam, which is deep and sluggish and home to perch and pike – which, one cannot help thinking, must make serious inroads into juvenile salmon stocks. A short distance above the dam, however, is the Linn of Barhoise and below this the Bladnoch offers delightful water of fine holding pools and fast runs that make fly fishing an altogether pleasant task. This character lasts downstream as far as Crows, where, unfortunately, the river reverts to its sluggish nature and perch and pike are again found in great numbers. However, this section does hold its share of salmon, particularly in the spring, and should not be disregarded. Finally, there is the lower section from Torhouse Mill down to the estuary. This is reminiscent of the water below the Linn, with good pools and runs for the fisherman.

### Season

*Salmon* 14 February to 31 October (best March–May and September–October).

### Fish and Fishing

The Bladnoch is very important to the fishing scene in the south-west of Scotland because it is one of the few Solway rivers to boast any sort of a spring run. Indeed, there are those who would argue that of all the Solway rivers the Bladnoch offers the best chance for early-season sport. The first salmon of the Bladnoch season may well be taken in February but, in a normal year,

*A 10 lb September salmon is safely ashore*

Bladnoch fishermen look to the end of March and through to May to provide their early-season sport.

As you might expect, spinning is productive in this early season and 9-foot rods, fixed-spool reels and silver, blue-and-silver or blue-and-pearl Devon minnows take a fair share of the catch. This is in contrast to late-season spinning, when the brown-and-gold and Yellow Belly have proved themselves time after time.

However, at least three sections offer holding pools and runs suitable for fly fishing. Popular flies include long-standing favourites such as the Hairy Mary and the Garry Dog. In the back end of September and October, as spawning time approaches, Bladnoch salmon may respond aggressively to a gold-and-orange fly, a popular choice being Dunkeld or Thunder and Lightning. A rod of 14 feet is adequate most of the time.

Given the all-important rainfall and decent water levels, sport will continue with summer salmon and grilse through the months of June and July. At this time of year, however, for a Solway river, the Bladnoch is sadly lacking in sea-trout. In fact, most authorities would write off the Bladnoch entirely as a sea-trout fishery, with very few of these fish ever being caught.

Finally, to close the Bladnoch salmon season, autumn runs of fish enter the river in September and October.

## Access

Much of the Bladnoch is in private ownership, but the Newton Stewart and District Angling Association leases a 3-mile stretch below Loch Maberry which can fish well later on in the season. Addresses are given above under the Cree.

Mochrum Park has three stretches of single-bank fishing, close to the sea. These are the Mochrum Park beat itself, with twelve pools described as 'good, open fly water'; another smaller stretch; and 2½ miles of single-bank fishing at High and Low Barness, which is only half a mile above tidal water. It should be noted, however, that all this fishing is normally reserved for guests staying at various cottages. For further details contact:

Mr Hayley
Foxen Lanehead Hall
Soyland
Ripponden
Yorkshire
*Telephone* 0422 822148

The Corsemalzie Hotel water has 24 pools on its 4-mile stretch. The spinner is used here a great deal until about the end of March, when the fly rod really comes into its own. The fishing is normally reserved for hotel guests, though spare rods may sometimes be available. As on Mochrum Park, shrimp and prawn are not allowed. The hotel also owns 8 miles of salmon fishing on the Tarff, a tributary of the Bladnoch. Contact:

Corsemalzie House Hotel
Port William
Newton Stewart
Dumfries and Galloway
*Telephone* 098 886254

## LUCE

The Luce, more correctly known as the Water of Luce, is formed by the joining of the Main Water of Luce and the Cross Water of Luce. The Main Water has been dammed to form Penwhirn Reservoir. Faced with compensation flow, this once-productive spate fishery has faded to a shadow of its former productivity. However, and thankfully for the main river, the Cross Water rises high in the Ayshire hills and takes in a not inconsiderable catchment area.

## Season

*Salmon and Sea-trout*   25 February to 31 October (best from July until end of season).

## Fish and Fishing

While salmon stocks in the Luce may be in the ascendancy, sea-trout have certainly suffered a decline. What sea-trout there are tend to run the Main Water, with catches being at their best in July and August, when some reasonable night fishing can be enjoyed on lower stretches. A rod of about 10 feet and traditional sea-trout flies, sizes 8 or 10, prove as useful here as they do on any Solway river.

Salmon run both tributaries following a spate, but there is a sad lack of holding pools in the Luce system. This has the effect that fish and fishermen tend to become concentrated and congested in the favourite spots. When spinning for salmon, a fairly small brown-and-gold Devon has proved its worth time after time. For fly fishing, the General Practitioner and various patterns of the Shrimp Fly are always worth a swim.

## Access

Stair Estates own almost the entire river. Some stretches may be available from time to time. Contact:

>   Stair Estate Office
>   Rephad
>   Stranraer
>   Dumfries and Galloway

Four miles above the village of Luce, The Stranraer District Angling Association controls an 8-mile stretch on the Cross Water. Permits to fish this stretch are available from various hotels in the district and:

>   Rodgersports
>   26 Charlotte Street
>   Stranraer
>   *Telephone* 0776 3996

# 2 Ayrshire Rivers and Lomond

## STINCHAR

The Stinchar, rivalled only by the Doon in recent seasons as the most productive salmon river in Ayrshire, has its source at Loch Linfern in the Carrick Forest. On its 20-mile northerly journey to the sea at Ballantrae it picks up two major tributaries, the Duisk and the Assel.

Loch Linfern is relatively small and there is no reservoir of water on the Stinchar, therefore it has all the characteristics of a spate river. This has been exacerbated by afforestation with its associated drainage schemes over much of the river's catchment area. Once the land is well dampened, as it tends to be in the prime months of September and October, even a short period of heavy rain will bring the Stinchar into flood. Equally, in just the same way as the rise is swift, so the river does not take long to fall to a good fishing height. On this point of spates, rainfall in Scotland can be very localized. It can fall, say, on the catchment of the Duisk

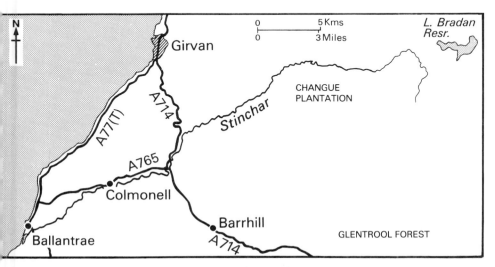

Map 5    *The Stinchar*

tributary, but not on that of the main river. The upper Stinchar, then, would remain clear, the Duisk would be in full spate, and the lower Stinchar would be in half spate.

Perhaps what sets Stinchar aside from its Ayrshire neighbours is the purity of its water. Many parts of Ayrshire have in the past been the scene of heavy industrialization, and the rivers of the county have suffered pollution, be it from disused coal mines or sewage. Now all Ayrshire rivers are cleaner. Stinchar, on the other hand, never suffered; it escaped the close proximity of major towns and industry and this factor and enlightened management of the salmon resource within the river have given it the reputation it enjoys today. But there is more to it than that because, on top of this, the Stinchar offers some of the finest water for fly fishing to be found in south-west Scotland – holding pools and fine streamy water, with the best of it lying from Pinwherry down to the sea.

## Season

25 February to 31 October (best September–October for salmon, May–August for sea-trout).

## Fish

Very few salmon enter the Stinchar in the opening months of the season, though an odd few may be taken in April or thereabouts. In summer the story can be rather different. As this is a spate river, summer prospects are entirely dependent upon rainfall but, given summer spates, brief bonanzas of sport with salmon and grilse may be expected from July onwards. Then, as rain and spates become more dependable towards the autumn, sport steadily builds in a fine crescendo during September and October.

Sea-trout take a back seat to salmon on the Stinchar. However, they are certainly about for those prepared to give them a try in the summer dusks. The best times for sea-trout are from May until August. May and June are the months to be looking for the maturer and larger class of sea-trout, whilst July and August can continue to show sport with a smaller class of fish.

## Fishing

The Stinchar rises but also falls quickly. A spate at dawn can have fined down to an excellent height and clarity for fishing the fly by noon. This factor, coupled with the fine, streamy nature of much of the Stinchar, means that the river is something of a fly fisherman's paradise. Indeed, many of its better-known and most popular stretches have a fly-only rule. On such beautiful water it seems a shame to dishonour river and fish with anything less than the fly, and this is what attracts so many of its regular fishing visitors.

*Tackle*

The Stinchar is far from being a large river. It can be covered quite adequately with a double-handed 14-foot carbon rod. In summer a single-handed rod of 10 feet is a good alternative for the smaller class of salmon fly, and will double for sea-trout.

As to the pattern of fly, for summer use there is little to rival the Stinchar Stoat. Take a standard Stoat's Tail with its black wing, hackle and body ribbed with gold, substitute an orange hackle for the black, and you have a Stinchar Stoat. It is something like a Thunder and Lightning, which is a very good alternative in a traditional dressing. Indeed, a good friend of mine who is an expert salmon catcher and Stinchar regular takes the similarity to the Thunder and Lightning a stage further by adding jungle-cock cheeks to his Stinchar Stoat, and does very well with the result.

Whilst there may be little to rival the Stinchar Stoat, there is the General Practitioner. This now widely popular fly was first tied by the late Colonel Esmond Drury. He was a regular visitor to the Stinchar and this fly, an imitation of a prawn, and the excellent long-shanked treble hooks he designed and named after himself are both popular legacies to the Stinchar. The fly does particularly well in a clearing water on the heels of a spate, fished deep on a sinking line. The pattern is carried in sizes ranging from a 2 down to a 10. Another popular fly for use on the Stinchar is the Garry Dog. Yet another is the Duke's Killer. This was first tried by the Duke of Wellington on the Knockdolian Estate, which belongs to the Duchess, some ten years ago. Basically, it is little more than a Stinchar Stoat but with the addition of a hot-orange chenille body. The first time the Duke gave it a swim, the new pattern, tied on a 2-inch Waddington shank, hooked four fish. Again, it has proved its worth in a clearing water over the years, and down to summer sizes as well as on the larger Waddingtons and tube flies.

The Stinchar's sea-trout fishing can be excellent, with the best numbers coming normally in July and August. Traditional Scottish sea-trout patterns and tactics will take their share of these game fish.

Finally, a word on spinning. Where and when the spinning rod is allowed, and for those who wish to use it, a 2-inch Devon minnow or a Toby of similar size can work well, as does a Mepps after a summer spate. An 8-foot spinning rod, fixed-spool reel and about 12-lb BS nylon complete the outfit.

## Access

As is the case on virtually all Scottish rivers, the good ones I mean, demand is always one step ahead of supply. It is not easy to get onto a beat on the Stinchar. You may have to be prepared to take a summer rod, pray for rain, and wait until a back-end week becomes vacant. But here are some of the places and people you might approach with serious inquiries.

Starting at the seaward end of the river, close to the sea-side village of the same name, there is the Ballantrae beat. This water, which takes in the tidal pools as well as the lowermost fresh, is fly-only. Fishing on this beat, which is for four guests, is let in conjunction with a fishing lodge. Vacancies are rare. Contact:

> R. Dalrymple
> Crailoch Farm
> Ballantrae
> Ayrshire
> *Telephone* 046 583 297

Further upstream, Kirkholm Farm has tickets for four rods on their stretch between Ballantrae and Colmonell. Contact:

> Mr Marshall
> Kirkholm Farm
> Ballantrae
> *Telephone* 046 583 297

Next up is the outstanding Knockdolian Estate Water. Do not expect many vacancies on a beat which produced more than 500 salmon in 1988 and nearly 700 in 1985. Accommodation is to be had in two fishing lodges, and, dependent upon the time of year at which you want to fish, you might just get lucky. Contact:

> Knockdolian Estate
> Alderside
> Colmonell
> Girvan
> Ayrshire
> *Telephone* 046 588 237

Above Colmonell is the Bardrochat Estate beat. This is single-bank fishing, and fly-only. Day tickets may be available. Contact:

R. Anderson
Oaknowe
Bardrochat Estate
Colmonell
Ayrshire
*Telephone* 046 588 202

Then there is the Darleoch Estate's beat. This again is fly-only, except that spinning will be allowed when the water level is above a certain height. Eight guests may fish, with day tickets being available up to the end of August. During the months of September and October, the peak salmon times, weekly tickets only. Contact, by telephone:

D. Overend
*Telephone* 046 588 214

## GIRVAN

One of the outstanding features of the Girvan is that, for such a small river, it has such a large number of tributaries. A number of authorities suggest Loch Bradan as the primary source. This loch was developed as a water supply in the early years of this century, with further enlargement works being carried out as recently as the 1970s. From the loch, the river flows north-west to Kirkmichael before turning south-west on its way to the sea at Girvan, an attractive Ayrshire coastal resort.

Down as far as Straiton the river would be better described as a moorland stream but below Straiton it opens out and swells to create good holding pools and streamy runs. Next there comes a rather sluggish and featureless stretch, from Crosshill to Dailly, caused, it is said, by 'land improvement work'. But this stretch does not last for too long because below Dailly the river enters the Blairquhan Estate, which contains some of the finest country in the county.

Thanks to the efforts of the District Salmon Fishery Board and an active improvement association, the Girvan is fast recovering after the disaster of the late seventies. Toxic waste had been building up in a disused colliery and, in August 1979, started to discharge itself into the river at a rate, it is said, of 500,000 gallons a day. The effect on returning populations of migratory fish can be imagined. Cleaning up the river, plus restocking from their own small hatchery, has done much to return the Girvan to its former state. Equally, up until recent times, bag netting was carried out on either side of the river mouth. This commercial operation has ceased. All those involved with the restoration and enhancement of the Girvan will take great pride in the fact that, in 1988, it enjoyed its best ever season since the fish-rich days of the early 1960s.

## Season

25 February to 31 October (best September–October for salmon, June–July for sea-trout).

## Fish and Fishing

Fishing on the Girvan follows very much the same pattern as on its neighbour, the Stinchar – nothing much to talk about in the early months, the potential for brief bursts of sport if given decent

*Safely in the net; the celebrations can begin*

summer rain, and finally a peak of sport in the two closing months of the season.

The nature of the sea-trout runs – early-summer sport with larger, mature fish, followed by smaller fish through to September – is also similar to the Stinchar.

Popular flies are also very much the same in sizes from 2½-inch tubes and Waddingtons for late-season work down to size 10 or even a 12 in summer, with the Stinchar Stoat, General Practitioner and Garry Dog all doing well. A traditional favourite, as on so many rivers of the south-west of Scotland, is the Brown Turkey. This is a straightforward strip-wing style of salmon fly. It has a cinnamon turkey wing, a black hackle and a body in three parts of, starting at the head, black, red and yellow seal fur, all ribbed with silver or gold. Some fly dressers add a tinsel tag of the same colour as the body ribbing, a gold pheasant crest for a tail and, in larger sizes, an underwing of teal and tippets.

On those beats which allow spinning, the same lures as described for the Stinchar are all that is required.

## Access

Carrick Angling Club have approximately 2 miles of fishing stretching upstream from Girvan harbour. Contact:

> J. Murray
> Fishing Tackle Dealer
> Dalrymple Street
> Girvan
> Ayrshire

Further upstream, the Bargany Estate's water is divided into four beats. Fly and spinning. Contact, by telephone:

> The Keeper's House
> *Telephone* 046 581 437

Above Dailly is the Kilkerran Estate stretch. Again, contact the keeper by phone:

> *Telephone* 06554 278

Last, but by no means least, there is the very picturesque Blairquhan Estate water, where the rule is fly or worm but not spinner. There are a good number of fine pools on this beat. Contact, again by phone:

> *Telephone* 065 57 259

## DOON

'Ye banks and braes o' bonnie Doon' are the words with which Robert Burns immortalized the scene he knew so well. Of course, he would not have recognised Loch Doon, nor its sluice and fish pass – though, if he had been a fisherman, he might have come to appreciate the compensation flow from the loch which maintains a steady flow while other spate rivers fade in summer droughts. It is but one of the factors that have raised the Doon to become Stinchar's real challenger for the title of the most productive salmon river in Ayrshire.

The Doon rises in Loch Doon in the Carrick Forest and enters just one mile south of Ayr. It flows through the heart of Burns Country – past Dalmellington, Patna, Dalrymple, Minishant and, most closely associated with Burns, Alloway.

### Season

11 February to 31 October (best September–October for salmon, May–August for sea-trout).

### Fish and Fishing

It seems to be the inevitable case that where any sort of dam or barrage is constructed on a river the spring run of salmon immediately suffers. Before the dam was constructed there was a significant spring run into the Doon. Salmon certainly used the fish pass and were, therefore, allowed access to the abundant spawning streams. However, it is one thing to get salmon to ascend an obstacle and quite another to get the resulting smolts to descend through the fish pass on their journey to the sea. This is all the more frustrating when we know of so many cases where young salmon placed by human hand above a natural obstruction such as a falls will descend happily and therefore allow man to maximize the river's spawning potential. Anyway, the effect of a dam – allied to the fact that it is, in general terms, the earliest running fish that push right on up into the headwaters while many autumn fish are content to spawn in the middle and lower reaches – is that the spring run can and often does suffer. And such has been the case on the Doon.

Therefore it is not until the first summer spates that Doon fishermen expect to see or catch a fish, but then, from June onwards, the Doon like other Ayrshire rivers falls into a pattern of brief bursts of sport with summer salmon and grilse before water

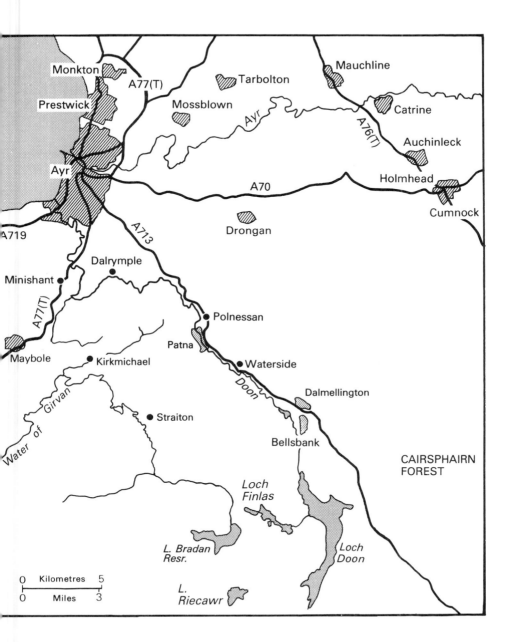

Map 6    *Doon and Ayr*

levels are more conducive to showing steady and often spectacular sport through the last two months of the season. And it comes as little surprise to discover that there is a great upsurge in sport once netting operations cease at the river mouth on 26 August.

While the salmon stocks are steadily improving on the Doon, it is sad to report that the same thing cannot be said for its sea-trout. Indeed, sea-trout stocks are suffering all up the west coast of Scotland. It is my opinion that it is high time we took a look at commercial fishery policy in coastal waters, and the grants made out of taxpayers' money to convert a substantial number of the Scottish fleet to take sandeel and other bait fish to be processed into fish meal. Already, besides sea-trout stocks, concern is being expressed for populations of sea birds which, quite simply, are finding it more and more difficult to find food. Is it not ironic that one of the final uses for fish meal is to fatten those flabby-fleshed rainbow trout that appear on supermarket shelves?

*Tackle*
None of these Ayrshire rivers is at all large and there is little need for a salmon rod of greater length than 14 feet. Even that could be considered a bit too long for summer use. An 8 foot spinning rod and fixed-spool reel completes the outfit except, perhaps, for a rather longer worming rod, if you wish.

**Access**

Access to the Doon is severely restricted. The fact is that nearly all the river is either in private hands or syndicated. From time to time, however, day tickets for the Skeldon Estate stretch may become available. This is a double-bank stretch with twelve named pools where six rods are let, normally in conjunction with two cottages. For details contact:

> The Estate Manager
> Skeldon Estate
> *Telephone* 0292 56656

In the vicinity of the village of Patna tickets can be available on the Drumgrange and Keir's Angling Club stretch of the Doon. Contact:

> Mr MacDonald
> Palace Bar Waterside Stores
> Dunaskin
> Ayrshire
> *Telephone* 0292 204

# AYR

The Ayr is the largest of Ayrshire's salmon rivers. Its source is away up on Wardlaw Hill between Muirkirk and New Cumnock, from where it runs 39 miles to the sea at Ayr. Its catchment area is extensive and, therefore, while it is certainly a spate river, it is not so 'flashy' as other Ayrshire rivers in this respect. In other words, spates on the Ayr take longer to get started after rain, and last that little bit longer as well. Spates on most Ayrshire rivers can be measured in terms of hours from the start of the rise to its height and eventual fall but, on the Ayr, it is more often a matter of days. In this respect, and others, the Ayr has been likened to the Nith, in terms of the salmon rivers of the south-west of Scotland.

Perhaps the most scenic stretch of the river is on the Stair and Falford stretches. Here there is a good variety of water with some interesting holding pools. But one note of caution for the wading angler. In the middle reaches parts of the river flow over a sandstone bed, and you must be careful where you are stepping.

Other than poaching and sniggling, the Ayr river suffers from two major factors that inhibit it from reaching its full potential. One is the large number of now redundant dams and weirs – an unwanted legacy of the Industrial Revolution. The majority do have fish passes but, even so, they act as a hindrance to fish on their upstream migration as well as concentrating them into areas where they can so easily fall prey to organized gangs of ruthless poachers. The effect of these gangs should never be underestimated.

The other problem that the Ayr faces is pollution. A great deal of this emanates from disused coal mines. Then there are sewage and other discharges.

If the problems of pollution, poaching and obstruction can be solved, there is little doubt that the Ayr has the potential to become a salmon river of very considerable worth. However, this is far from saying that the Ayr, even in its present state, is not worthy of consideration.

## Season

11 February to 31 October (best September–October for salmon, June–July for sea-trout).

## Fish and Fishing

Beside the effects already mentioned, the scourge of UDN, the salmon disease, was particularly hard on Ayr's stock of spring and summer salmon. Although a few fish may be taken in the lower stretches at the start of the season, the spring run has never really recovered. Summer salmon and grilse have fared far better and, given the essential rainfall to raise summer water levels, the Ayr may expect runs of fish from June onwards. But it is really not until the rain becomes more predictable and the nets are lifted towards the end of August that the Ayr shows real sport. Through September and October, local and visiting anglers will find the best of the season's sport, especially in the middle and upper reaches.

The spinner and worm are the most popular methods with locals. For the spinner, black-and-gold and Yellow Belly minnows are successful, as is a Zebra Toby. Some favour a big Mepps, size 3, in gold or copper. When fishing the fly, they might choose a 14-foot rod. Favourite patterns of fly include the Brown Turkey, the Blue Charm, the Stinchar Stoat and the General Practitioner. Sizes obviously vary according to the time of year. In summer, once the water has fallen and cleared, small flies work best. Try a size 8 or 10 on a floating or sink-tip line. Later on, when the hint of winter is in the air, try larger patterns of tube flies and Waddingtons. Flies with some yellow, red and orange can work well, such as the Garry Dog.

**Access**

Ayr is a noted seaside resort with plenty to keep the non-fishing members of the family happy and occupied. It also has a number of tackle shops which sell tickets for the town stretch. Otherwise contact:

> Director of Finance
> Kyle and Carrick District Council
> Town Buildings
> Ayr

Tickets for the Mauchline Ballochmyle Angling Club's water at Mauchline can be obtained from:

> The Post Office
> High Street
> Mauchline
> Ayrshire

At Auchinleck, tickets for the Auchinleck Angling Association's water may be had from:

J. McColm
21 Milne Avenue
Auchinleck
Ayrshire

# IRVINE AND GARNOCK

The northernmost of the Ayrshire salmon rivers are the Irvine and Garnock. They share a common estuary at the town of Irvine, another Ayrshire coastal resort which has plenty to keep non-fishing family members occupied and happy.

The Irvine itself has its source close to Drumclog in the county of Lanarkshire, about 25 miles from the sea. On its journey, it travels through great contrasts of scenery – agricultural, industrial and the ever-growing urban sprawl of Glasgow's commuter belt. Small wonder that pollution can be a problem from time to time, though things have improved wonderfully in recent times and, with the laudable efforts of a local improvement association, the Irvine can now be relied upon to show fairly consistent sport. Thankfully, the growing numbers of returning salmon do not have to face commercial netsmen on their arrival back at the river of their birth.

The Garnock rises east of Largs, barely 15 miles from the estuary, which makes it the smallest of Ayrshire's salmon rivers. It flows through similar contrasts of landscape to the Irvine. Unfortunately, however, despite the work of its own improvement association, the Garnock suffers very heavily, rather than just spasmodically, from pollution. As a result there have been some devastating fish kills in recent years. It says a great deal about the resilience of salmon stocks that any numbers have survived, but survived they have and, although heavy bags cannot be expected, the Garnock has its occasional brief moments of glory.

## Season

25 February to 31 October (best September–October for salmon, June–July for sea-trout).

## Fish and Fishing

Fishing on the Irvine and Garnock closely follows the pattern of sport found on all Ayrshire's rivers. Very few if any fish can be expected before June. Summer sport is heavily dependent upon rainfall. May and June can show sport with mature sea-trout while smaller fish will run the river in July and August.

Again, the popular flies are such patterns as the Brown Turkey, the Blue Charm, the Stinchar Stoat and the General Practitioner, or a Shrimp pattern in sizes 8 and 10 in summer and up to 2-inch tubes and Waddingtons in autumn, while, as on most of the south-wests's autumn salmon rivers, size 4 and 6 flies can still prove deadly through till the end of October. It can be a mistake, at times, to fish too large a fly at the back end of the season.

## Access

There are a large number of outlets for tickets on these two rivers. Most local tackle shops and a number of post offices can sell you a ticket.

## LOCH LOMOND

'The bonnie, bonnie banks of Loch Lomond' but let us get one or two facts straight from the start. First, the song was written by a young Jacobite prisoner thinking of his home and true love on the night before his execution, so sing it with a tear in your eye, rather than a swagger in your step! Second, if you have only travelled up the western shore on the busy road where traffic crawls along in a queue of lorries and caravans, do not think that you know the true character of the loch. Out in a boat, drifting the islands and shorelines where buzzards soar and deer come down to drink, is the only way to get the true feel of the place. Third, realize that Loch Lomond is a tremendous fishery but one that writes its own set of rules. Men who have spent their fishing lives on the loch will tell you that they have only begun to scratch at the surface of its secrets.

Loch Lomond is very largely a product of the Ice Age. There is a geographical fault line running from Balmaha across to Arden. And the loch is very different south of the village of Luss. Above Luss, it is steep-banked, narrow and deep. Below Luss, the loch and its shores broaden out, the loch is dotted with islands and, the closer you approach Balloch and the southern shore, so the water gets even shallower.

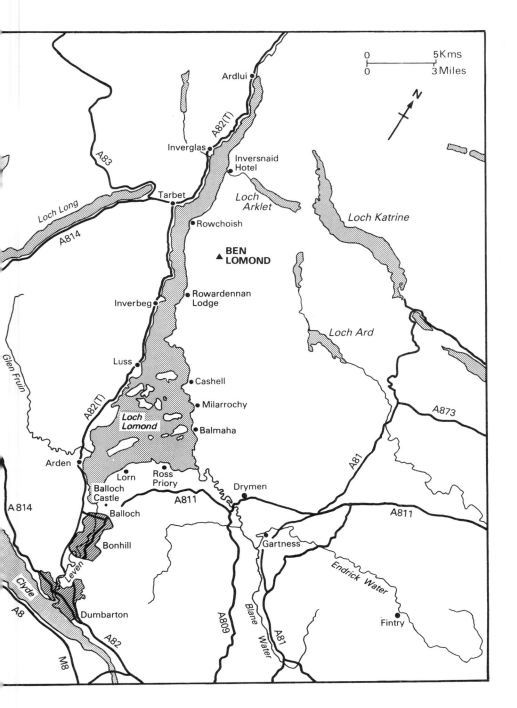

Map 7   *Loch Lomond*

This is an important point. Salmon show a preference for shallow water in any loch, between about 4 and 8 feet being to their liking. Sea-trout, on the other hand, while prepared to rest in such shallow water, will also be found in 20 feet and more.

Glacial deposits left after the Ice Age also create the basis of the great banks of silt, sand and bounders which again create shallower water. The Pilot Bank above Ross is a typical example, while others, such as the Endrick Bank at the mouth of the Endrick river, have been fortified by river silt over tens upon hundreds of centuries.

And so Loch Lomond may have the appearance of an unchanging, endless scene. But things are rather different. The fact of the matter is that many of the finest drifts and bays described in a number of books on the loch written at the start of this century have been changed out of all recognition. A barrage was built at Balloch where the loch empties into the Leven river. This effectively transformed the loch into a highly significant water supply for the needs of central Scotland, but it had the effect of 'drowning' many of the best known drifts under many extra feet of water. But anglers learn to adapt and, slowly, they learnt how the fish had changed their traditional resting places in the loch.

Other effects of the barrage are considered under the section on the Leven. As this is the river up which all Lomond salmon and sea-trout must run, they are obviously of very great significance.

**Season**

11 February to 31 October.

**Fish and Fishing**

Lomond fishing means boat fishing. It is an enormous water and the bank angler cannot even hope to make an impact.

*Early Season*
The Lomond season opens in February but, in a normal season, the first salmon to be taken off the loch normally falls in March. And it will normally have been found somewhere along the southern shore, between Balloch and Balmaha.

Very few Lomond regulars would even dream of fishing the fly this early in the season. In fact, they would look at you sideways if you were even to suggest it. No, the standard Lomond tactic in the early months of the season is to troll. This involves trailing a team of natural or artificial lures behind a slow-moving boat.

Standard practice is to fish three rods and lures. The rods will be of the spinning type and be fitted with fixed-spool or multiplier reels. The inner and outer rods will be in the 9–10-foot class, set in the fashion of outriggers to carry the lures about 25 yards behind the boat – a little less for the inner rod, closest to the shore, and a little more for the outer rod. The third rod, which trails a lure directly behind the boat and on a shorter line of about 15 yards, is a shorter and stiffer affair and, hence, is known as the 'poker'.

What lures to try? Although natural baits have fallen out of favour as being fiddly and time-wasting on most waters, on Lomond they remain extremly popular. The golden sprat is the out-and-out favourite, with a red sprat held in reserve for misty days. Lomond regulars even go to the extent of making their own spinning mounts to ensure that the sprat maintains its action at the slowest speeds, but these designs are closely kept secrets. They troll very slowly, the outboard barely ticking over, and concentrate on fishing water of between 5 and 8 feet in depth. This depth is most productive at any time of the season so far as trolling is concerned.

Towards the end of May even the most die-hard traditionalists will accept that the artificial lure can now work every bit as well as the natural. Favourites include the 18 g Toby, Rapalas and the incredible Kynoch Killer. The Kynoch looks something like an ice-cream cone with a treble hook mount slipped into its mouth and out of the side. As will be imagined, it fishes in a highly erratic manner, darting and weaving from side to side. Fish it on the short line and poker rod with maybe a Toby on the outer and a Rapala on the inner rod, to cover the options.

When a salmon takes, simply steer out into the loch towards deeper water and, with luck on your side, the salmon will follow like a dog on a lead. This gives time to wind up the spare lures and clear the way for action stations. And action there will be just as soon as you pick up the last rod and give the fish some stick!

*Fly Fishing*
At some time during May, Lomond fishermen will be looking to make a start with their fly rods. Trolling still continues, of course, with slightly smaller lures, but from now till the end of the season is when the fly rod can really score.

In choosing a rod, the fisherman must understand that on Lomond, as on virtually all salmon and sea-trout lochs, the standard practice is to fish a team of wet flies, and to concentrate on 'scuttering' the top dropper or bob fly on the water surface. This style is best effected with a fairly short line and long rod of 10–12 feet, which is raised to the vertical to bring the fly up to the surface.

Salmon do not like the bob fly to be moving too fast but for sea-trout it can hardly be moving fast enough on some days. This is the general rule but, as always in the pursuit of migratory species, there are plenty of exceptions to any rule we might care to make. If the fish are proving reluctant to move to the scuttered bob, try casting a longer line, retrieving in long, smooth draws, and only raise the bob fly to the surface for the last couple of yards of the retrieve.

Standard salmon and sea-trout patterns such as the Black Pennell, Wickham's, Peter Ross, Mallard and Claret, Dunkeld, and so on, will all take their quota of Lomond fish. However, there are a good number of favourite local patterns. Indeed, ask just about any regular Lomond fly fisherman if he has a secret favourite of his own and he will probably be happy to admit to its existence. And each one will be different. Some of the local favourites, however, have become quite well known.

The Turkey and Gold, or Ian Wood, is perhaps the most famous of Lomond flies to use on the bob when after salmon. In its standard form it has a white-tipped turkey wing, a gingery hackle, a gold body, and a golden pheasant crest tail. As with all Lomond flies, tie it on the sparse side. Another great Lomond bob fly is the Golden Olive. This has a hen pheasant wing and a palmered ginger hackle over golden–olive seal fur ribbed with oval gold. It is an excellent fly for bringing a sea-trout to the surface, and is normally tied on a size 6 hook.

The Mallard and Gold has a bronze mallard wing and a turn of blue hackle at the throat in front of a palmered red cock hackle over a gold body with gold rib and a golden pheasant crest tail. Its sister, the Mallard and Silver, is virtually the same except that the body and rib are silver instead of gold. Either of these Mallard patterns is excellent for the middle or tail positions on the cast, in sizes 8 or 10. Incidentally, a Mallard and Yellow can prove outstanding on the bob.

It is often tricky to choose a fly for the middle position when fishing three flies on the cast. To mention just one more Lomond favourite, the Burton can prove its worth in this respect. The Burton is a variation on the Brown Turkey – a great favourite on many a west coast river. The wing is cinnamon turkey and the tail a golden pheasant crest. The standard hackle is black and this has a body made up of equal segments of black, red and yellow seal fur, with the black closest to the head. One variant on this theme has the usual wing and tail but a blue hackle and blue, red and yellow seal fur. The body, in both flies, is ribbed with oval silver. Some fly dressers will tie in an underwing of teal and golden pheasant tippets.

These are just a few flies to try on Lomond. Other great favourites that I would not set sail without are a Silver Invicta and a Dark Mackerel. A full range of Lomond flies and a great deal of excellent advice on fishing Lomond will be found in the late Bill McEwan's book *Angling on Lomond*. A great book and a great fisherman – the drifts and shores of Lomond will never be the same without him. Incidentally, it says a great deal about Loch Lomond that at least four books have been written specifically about the place, as well as a number of other publications in which Lomond controls a near-monopoly on the writer's pen. But Bill's is the most recent and therefore most relevant of them all – an essential read for any fisherman planning his first, tenth or hundredth trip to the Big Loch.

As an alternative to the wet fly, the Lomond fisherman may try dapping. Indeed, the method continues to grow in popularity with regulars. This, no doubt, owes a great deal to a shift in species emphasis. In the old days, Lomond tended to be fished specifically for its salmon, with sea-trout being regarded as an added bonus. Nowadays, on the other hand, certainly after the close of May, it is the sea-trout that has come to be regarded as the Lomond fisherman's chief quarry, and it is the salmon that is the added bonus. And, you see, while dapping will certainly rise salmon and to a greater extent grilse, it is really best seen as a method for tempting sea-trout up to the surface from their deeper lies.

Equally, dapping tackle is straightforward and relatively inexpensive, and therefore always worth carrying. Telescopic dapping rods of about 15 feet in length, such as those produced by Shakespeare Tackle, are widely popular. A standard fly reel is used but, in place of the fly line, the spool is filled with braided backing. A length of about 20 feet of dapping floss is attached to the backing, loop to loop. And at the other end of the floss, about 4 feet of 12-lb nylon is attached, again loop to loop. All that remains is to attach the dapping fly.

Dapping flies come in all shapes and sizes. Perhaps the most commonly used is a beefed up version of the Black Pennell. Tied on a size 6 or 4 low-water salmon hook, it will have about ten stiff-fibred cock hackles tied in to occupy the forward half of the body. To increase its floatation, it is then smeared or sprayed with floatant.

Dapping is an art of the wind. With the rod tip pointing towards the heavens, the light floss line and fly sail out on the wind. Line is paid out until, with the rod now held at about 20 degrees to the vertical, it is possible to drop the fly gently on the waves, with the line not touching the water surface. Some dappers hold their fly almost static. Others prefer to give it some life, making it trip along the surface from side to side. This is the method that I find best where sea-trout are concerned. Long periods of hard concentration are rewarded when a dashing sea-trout erupts from the water beneath the fly. But I must warn you that dapping is a frustrating business at times. There are days when perhaps only one out of six fish risen are hooked!

**Where to Fish**

As I have said, people have written books describing the best ways and places to drift your boat in pursuit of Lomond salmon and sea-trout. The late Bill McEwan's book is stuffed with such advice. If you do not get a copy of this book, you will have to rely on local advice, and keeping a weather eye open for where the experienced fishermen are headed. Do not get in their way, of course, and never cut across their drifts. Travel well back in their wakes rather than in their shadows. There is a great tradition of lunch time ashore on the islands and bays of Lomond. Glasgow and its people have a long tradition for their open hospitality and, if approached in the right way, will 'crack' away about the fish and fishing and, if you admit to being a new boy, will often prove to be a fount of knowledge and wisdom as to whether you might try Inch Moan, Inch Cruin or Inch Fad, or tell you that they have heard of fish at Ireland or Darroch. And those who hire out the boats for fishing on Lomond have a finger on the pulse of who is catching what, and on what, where and when.

**Access**

Loch Lomond Angling Improvement Association controls the fishing, and does all it can to ensure that it maintains its high reputation in terms of quality and quantity of fish caught. Permits can be obtained from:

R. A. Clement
LLAIA Secretary
St Vincent Place
Glasgow
*Telephone* 041 221 0068

There are a number of places situated at various points around the loch where you can hire a boat and obtain permits. The best-known of these is:

MacFarlane and Sons
Balmaha
*Telephone* 036 087 214

## RIVERS LEVEN AND ENDRICK

Salmon run up the Leven in order to enter Loch Lomond. Having entered the loch, a fair percentage of the salmon and sea-trout runs will make their way to the mouth of the Endrick, a main feeder river into the loch, and run up it in order to spawn. Other tributaries include the Falloch at the top end of the loch and, on its western shore, the Inveruglas Water, Douglas, Finlas and Fruin, but none of these has the conditions to attract more than a few sea-trout to run. And so, certainly from the point of view of salmon

*The roll cast can be useful in situations like this where trees overhang the bank*

and sea-trout fishing, it is acceptable to ignore virtually all rivers and streams associated with the loch except for the Leven and the Endrick.

## Season

As for Loch Lomond.

## Leven Fish and Fishing

There are some excellent pools in the the Leven although, perhaps surprisingly, it is relatively slow-flowing. Speed and depth do vary enormously, however, due to the barrage constructed at Balloch, where the Leven flows out of Loch Lomond. The rule as to flow is, or certainly was, that compensation flow into the Leven must not fall below 130 million gallons a day. In addition to this, a freshet will be created at least once in every thirty-day period by the release of 1,000 million gallons. The timing of these freshets is decided in conjunction with fishing interests.

To put this into perspective, however, it has to be remembered that 130 million gallons per day flowing down a river is not such a great amount. Before the barrage was erected, rates of flow of up to 800 million gallons per day were common, and best fishing heights were found when the Leven flowed at between 250 and 800 million gallons. Under compensation flow, therefore, it could be said that, most of the time, the river is flowing too low and then, when a freshet is allowed, it is just too big.

However, catch the Leven at a good height and it certainly can yield excellent support. As I have said, it has some really good pools, and salmon can be expected from February or March onwards. Any month from April through to the close of the season in October can produce good catches, but July usually ends up by easing out into the lead. Somewhere between 200 and 250 salmon are taken each season.

As you might expect, the sea-trout fishing can be of a very high standard. Again, they can come at any time from April to October, but the best of the sport normally comes in the summer months of July, August and September, with total catches for an average year being around the 1,500 mark.

Incidentally, it would be a mistake to think that all Leven salmon and grilse are bound for the loch. There is clear evidence that a good proportion of them spawn in the river below the barrage, though this is no real obstacle to their upstream progress. Sea-trout, on the other hand, seldom spawn in the Leven.

The Leven fishing is controlled by the Loch Lomond Angling Improvement Association and this is significant in how it is fished. Whilst tickets relating specifically to the Leven can be purchased, full membership of the association entitles members to fish Loch Lomond, the Leven and most of the Endrick, as well as the Fruin, the Luss Water and the lower Falloch. What happens, therefore, is not really surprising. As the late Bill McEwan summed it up: 'Well, Crawford, the river fishing can be excellent, but it pays to keep working away at the loch until you hear conditions on the river are just right. Then I moor the boat and motor down for a few casts.'

## Endrick Fish and Fishing

The Endrick rises in West Stirlingshire and flows west to its meeting with Loch Lomond just south of Balmaha. The upper part of the river can virtually be ignored, unless you think that salmon and sea-trout are capable of negotiating the 90-foot falls known as the Loup o' Fintry!

From the Loup down to the loch is a distance of about 20 miles. The upper part of this stretch offers fine pools and gravel spawning beds, but, for the fish, it is not that easily reached. Apart from a weir with a fish pass, there are more falls downstream, known as the Pot of Gartness. It takes a determined fish and the right height of water to get through the Pot. Below the Pot, the Endrick is joined by the Blane, its major tributary. The junction pool is a popular place with experienced Endrick fishermen, and is known as the Meetings Lynn.

Below Drymen, the lower section of the Endrick flows through rich woodlands and soft meadowland. Obviously, this leads to a fairly sluggish flow, but this stretch can fish well for all that.

It requires a spate to bring the Endrick into good fishing order, and to draw fish up from the loch. The best of the sport can be expected from June onwards though, in a very dry summer, it may be that not much happens before September and October. Obviously, salmon and sea-trout find it no hardship to rest in the loch, fairly close to the mouth of the river, and wait for rain and rising water levels.

In a reasonable year, you might expect something in the region of 500 sea-trout to be taken off the Endrick. The average weight of these fish will be in the region of 2½ lb but the Endrick can produce its share of 10-pounders and, occasionally, a lucky fisherman enjoys a night's sport with sea-trout to an average weight of 4 or 5 lb.

A catch of about 100 Endrick salmon would be typical for an average season. Again, their size is variable, with an average weight of about 7 lb, but with a few scaling in at the 20 lb mark. These bigger fish, incidentally, are nearly always found below the Pot of Gartness.

Anybody planning to fish the Endrick for its sea-trout might like to read Dr William B. (Bill) Currie's book *A Game-Fisher's Year*. He devotes a chapter or two to describing his conversion to the sunk-line technique of sea-trout fishing, inching back a duet of standard wet flies on a deeply sunk line, and all related to a private Endrick beat. Inspirational stuff, added to which is a description of the capture of a 13-lb Endrick sea-trout on a size 8 Wickham's Fancy!

## Access

For further details of both the Leven and Endrick contact the Secretary of the Loch Lomond Angling Improvement Association:

Messrs R. A. Clement & Co
29 St Vincent's Place
Glasgow
*Telephone* 041 221 0068

# 3 The West Coast From Kintyre to Mull

## EACHAIG AND LOCH ECK

Situated in the county of Argyll, the Eachaig is a short river of only 4½ miles draining Lock Eck into the head of the Holy Loch, with its naval bases. Short it may be, but it is also highly productive in terms of salmon and sea-trout, particularly since the commercial netting operations have ceased.

### Season

16 February to 31 October.

### Fish and Fishing

It would not be a mistake to consider the Eachaig–Eck system as primarily a sea-trout fishery, but one that can at times provide excellent sport with salmon. Besides the sheer numbers of sea-trout that it can produce, the Eachaig has a fine reputation as the producer of outsized sea-trout. It is fairly early days since the netting ceased but, when they were in operation, sea-trout of 20 lb were caught. I do not know what the current rod and line record for the system may be but, certainly, a sea-trout of 15 lb was caught in the late 1970s.

The fishing does not really get under way until June and then continues through the summer months, with August and September often being outstanding.

This pattern of fish catching is much the same on Loch Eck, as you would expect above what is such a relatively short river. The loch, which is about 6 miles long, is for the most part narrow and deep. Therefore, while the fly and dap can score, most fish – certainly most salmon – are taken on trolled lures such as the Rapala and the Kynoch Killer.

### Access

The Eachaig is now owned by Salar Properties, a company specializing in the sale of timeshares in perpetuity. Not all the weeks have been sold on this basis, however, and it is still possible to rent a week's fishing at certain times. Contact:

> Salar Properties
> Lochloy House
> Nairn
> IV12 5LE
> *Telephone* 0667 55355

Permission to fish Loch Eck – which, incidentally, holds trout, char and powan as well as salmon and sea-trout – can be obtained from the Whistlefield Inn. There are seven boats and a gillie is available. Contact:

> The Whistlefield Inn
> Loch Eck
> by Dunoon
> Argyll
> *Telephone* 036 986 250

## FYNE

The flow of water in the Fyne has been permanently reduced on a number of occasions in recent decades. In 1950 both of its upper tributaries were diverted as part of a hydroelectric scheme. Then in 1955 another of its tributaries was diverted for the same purpose in another scheme. And a reservoir was formed on the headwaters to provide a reserve of water to supply a power station. Such things may seem crazy to us fishermen, but the nation requires its electricity, so there we are.

It can be fairly said that, in the modern age, the Fyne features a totally artificial flow that is almost entirely dependent on compensation waters. And yet the Fyne is still a good producer of fish.

### Season

15 February to 31 October (best late June–August).

### Fish and Fishing

The Fyne sees small numbers of large salmon entering the river in April and May after the water level has been so arranged as to attract them to run. The main runs, however, come in the period

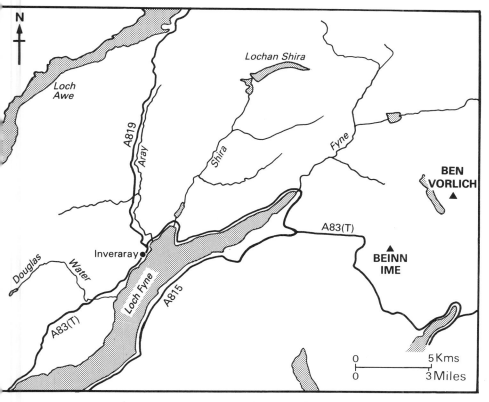

Map 8   *Rivers Fyne, Aray, Shira and Douglas*

from late June to August. Most of these fish are grilse, but there will be a fair proportion of larger salmon swimming with them.

The river is divided into four beats, in addition to tidal stretch which is available on a day–ticket basis. A number of the better pools have been improved still further by the erection of weirs.

How many fish are caught on the Fyne? Well, I simply cannot say, but at least one authority has suggested that the catch is not as high as it might be. When Derek Mills and Neil Graesser said of the Fyne in their book *The Salmon Rivers of Scotland* that in recent times the Fyne had been let to tenants 'who have more enthusiasm than skill', they were, in fact, doing little more than echoing the thoughts and words of many a Scottish fishing proprietor or gillie. And it has to be agreed that while twenty, thirty and more years ago there were a lot fewer people chasing salmon, they were, as a general rule, rather more skilled at the game! But I think it is perhaps a little unfair of Mills and Graesser to single out the tenants of the Fyne as *prime* examples of those who 'could do better'.

Some worming may be allowed on the river at various times, but no spinning is allowed. As one other West Coast rivers, a long rod is not really needed, and a standard selection of tried and trusted fly patterns should see you through – Hairy Mary, Stoat Tail, Munro Killer, Shrimp Fly, and the like.

## Access

The river is controlled by two estates, both of which are perhaps best approached by a telephone call to determine what fishing may be available. Contact:

Ardkinglas Estate
*Telephone* 04996 217

Cairndow Estate
*Telephone* 04996 284

## ARAY, SHIRA AND DOUGLAS

These are three small spate rivers, all entering the sea at the head of Loch Fyne, close to Inveraray.

The Aray starts its life as a rock–girt stream flowing through moorland in the area of Taynafead. Farther down its glen, the Aray grows in stature to create good salmon and sea–trout holding water that will interest the fisherman. This part of the river is heavily wooded, and the ability to Spey, roll or steeple cast becomes a definite advantage. Finally, the river enters the park surrounding Inveraray Castle to create an almost unique setting for fishing, with ornamental gardens, ornate bridges and man-made stepping stones as a backdrop.

Because of afforestation, this spate river has a tendency to rise and fall rapidly.

The Shira has been subjected to development for the generation of hydroelectricity. Lochan Shira leads to Lochan Sron Mor and, from here downstream, the river is subjected to compensation flow, and it is thus that it flows to Loch Shira, which is, in reality, little more than a bay in Loch Fyne. On the way, the river flows into Dubh Loch, which is significant from the fishing point of view, and empties into Loch Shira down the tidal Gearr Abhain.

Finally, there is the 12-mile-long Douglas Water. This is a rocky little river with plenty of waterfalls. One of these falls, about 3 miles above the saltwater of Loch Fyne, acts as a barrier to ascending fish. This confines any salmon and sea-trout that run the

Douglas to its lower ten pools, the best of which, perhaps, is the Roman Bridge Pool.

## Season

The season may be regarded as running from May to September.

## Fishing

The Aray enjoys three main runs of salmon. These normally occur in May; then the bulk of the salmon and grilse run in late June and July; and, finally, to round off the Aray season, salmon will run again in September. Surprisingly, perhaps, very few sea-trout enter the Aray and, as they are virtually never seen above tidal waters, it can only be presumed that these are fish destined to run and spawn in some other stream.

These rivers are all small and, although many fishermen prefer to use a 12- or 13-foot double-handed rod, many get their greatest enjoyment from a single-handed rod of about 10 feet in length. As for flies, these will generally be small and you could do a lot worse than to stick with traditional West Coast favourites such as the Hairy Mary, the Blue Charm, the Stoat's Tail or, in traditional patterns, the Thunder and Lightning, which fishes so well in a falling water.

Shira fish tend to rest in Dubh Loch, just above the tide, until autumn, when the river above can come into its own. So seek the salmon, grilse and sea-trout in the loch during the months of July and August and don't think much about the river until September. Of course, it should also be noted that at any time after July a heavy spate in the Shira is likely to draw fish up and out of the loch. Equally, or so I have been told, a big tide may occasionally encourage fish to run back into the sea. The tidal nature of Dubh Loch and Gearr Abhain is clearly illustrated by the occasional presence of grey mullet, boiling and rising in the shallows.

## Access

Daily or weekly tickets to fish any of the three rivers or Dhubh Loch may be available from time to time. Contact:

The Factor
Argyll Estates
Cherry Park
Inveraray
Argyll
*Telephone* 0499 2203

# THE KINTYRE PENINSULA

Kintyre, the long peninsula running from Lochgilphead down to Campbeltown, has an atmosphere that is all its own, away from the mundane things of everyday life. It also has a number of fisheries which, in their time, can yield sport with salmon and sea-trout. None of these fisheries can be counted as household names, and the lochs and rivers are small. You could take a 13-foot double-handed rod along with you, but you might be just as well served with a single-hander of 10-11 feet, which would serve equally well for sea-trout or, if the migratory fish were not obliging, to fish a team of wet flies for trout. A selection of traditional favourite salmon and sea-trout flies in small summer sizes should serve you well in this area.

## Best Months

May, June and September.

To mention a few of the possibilities:

## The Lussa

The Lussa empties into the sea near Peniver, about 4 miles north of Campbeltown on the eastern shore of the peninsula. Much of the river has been virtually ruined for fishing by the erection of a dam on Lussa Loch without any provision for compensation flow. How the water gets from the Loch to the power station is a rather complicated story involving aqueducts and pipelines but, for our needs as fishermen, it is probably sufficient to know that the best of the fishing is in the lowermost stretches. Some 70 salmon and about 200 sea-trout might be expected off the Lussa in a reasonable season.

## Machrihanish Water

This flows into the sea surrounded by the famed sands of Machrihanish Bay on the west coast, but close to Campbeltown. It has produced salmon up to 20 lb on occasions, and the fish can come in fair numbers as well. Somebody must own the river but, although I would never advocate that you should fish without permission, I am told that when the river is right and the fish are running the whole population, local and visitor alike, will be out with their worming rods.

In a rather similar vein, both the Breakerie and Conie Waters at the southern tip of Kintyre are fished with a *laissez-faire* approach. Indeed, I was told by one wit who had visited the area that, if anybody, you should perhaps ask the local poachers for permission, lest you upset them by interfering with their netting operations.

## Carradale

This delightful little river also gets its share of attention from poachers but it can fish well on the heels of a spate. As on so much of the West Coast, local inquiry will point you in the right direction to seek permission to have a cast – in this case from the keeper on Carradale Estate.

## Claonaig

The fishings on this river, which flows out on the east coast of Kintyre at Skipness, are owned by the Skipness Estate. It is a small spate river that can yield sport with sea-trout from June onwards, and salmon from July onwards. The fishing is let to visitors staying in estate cottages.

These are just a few of the fishings available on the Kintyre peninsula but in describing them I have perhaps given enough of a feeling for how salmon and sea-trout fishing is regarded and conducted in these parts. If you would like to find out more, you can seek advice from:

A. P. MacGrory
Main Street
Campbeltown
Kintyre
*Telephone* 0586 52132

Alternatively, try phoning the Tourist Information Office (*telephone* 0586 52056).

## ADD

It is tempting to include the Add along with the rest of the rivers in Kintyre. However, along with the Barr – which, since it is kept strictly private, I have not troubled to mention – it is perhaps one of the best rivers in the Kintyre district. In a good season, it might just yield more than 200 salmon.

The Add is formed by the joining together of a number of burns and, in its upper and middle reaches, it has a steep, rocky fall. Then it enters flatter ground, close to the Crinan Canal, and eventually the flow falls right away. Indeed, the last 2 miles of the river are tidal.

Virtually all West Coast rivers are highly dependent on spates, and are therefore 'flashy' in their character. The Add is made all the more so by extensive afforestation, and, again like so many of these waters, it has been tapped for the generation of hydroelectricity. A strange character indeed – flashy spates alternating with minimal compensation flow!

Fishing for salmon and grilse is normally best in July and August, and it takes place on three beats into which the river is divided – Minard, Kirnan and Poltalloch. Poltalloch is the lowermost beat as well as normally being the most productive, though Kirnan often manages to run it a close second.

## Access

For details of fishing that may be available contact:

H. MacArthur
The Tackle Shop
Lochnell Street
Lochgilphead
Argyll

## AWE

The River Awe drains mighty Loch Awe into the sea. Half loch and half river down the narrow top of the Pass of Brander, the river – when in its natural state – then picked up momentum for its short 3-mile journey into saltwater Loch Etive, not far east of Oban. The river is remembered as a roaring stream of fast-flowing pools and deep, rocky runs – somewhat similar to the rivers of Norway. But I have written 'in its natural state' and 'remembered' because, quite simply, this once truly great salmon river has been severely tampered with. A near-60-foot-high barrage was built across the river in the early sixties. This barrage has severely affected not only the Awe but also its fish and fishing. But, as we shall see, it has not all been for the worse.

*Fighting the current and the rocky bottom with chest waders and staff*

## Season

11 February to 15 October (best April–June and September).

## Fish and Fishing

The early fishing history of the Awe is one of giant salmon. It was upon its ability to produce outstanding sizes of salmon that its reputation was founded. Major A. W. Huntington caught a 57-pounder on a 3/0 Mar Lodge in 1921, and a 51-pounder in 1930. Mrs Huntington had a 55-pounder. A salmon of 56 lb took 2½ hours to land in 1923 and, in 1913, a 53-pounder was taken on a Childers fly. And there are a number of other 50-lb fish, indicating that there will have been even greater numbers of 40-pounders, exceptional numbers of 30-pounders, and so many 20-pounders as to be only worth passing mention. But not today. With the passing of the old Awe on the erection of the barrage its giant salmon went. Nowadays it is only on a very, very occasional basis that this river can produce a 30-pounder.

The plus point of the barrage, however, is concerned with the fact that the Awe is only the first leg in what is a very much larger system. The fish that run the Awe are running on to 23-mile-long Loch Awe, and on to the Orchy. Before the barrage was erected there was a definite tendency for the salmon to run quickly through the Awe so that, in times past, serious fishing did not really start until some time in June. The Awe fisherman of thirty and forty years ago would have been dumbfounded to learn that best times on the Awe are now reckoned to be from April to June, and again in September.

Incidentally, one might question why it is that the Awe fishing does not continue up till the legal closing date for the season on 15 October. The fact of the matter is that, while large numbers of salmon might undoubtedly be caught, the season is closed at the end of September by general consent among the proprietors. This river does not have a true run of autumn salmon and, therefore, this should be seen as a laudable effort to avoid the killing of gravid fish that are on the verge of spawning.

The fishing on the Awe is by fly only. Large tubes will be used in the opening months of the season, fished off a sinking line and generally a 15-foot carbon rod. Summer sport will be carried out with a floating, intermediate or sink-tip line, depending upon the individual's fancy, and fairly small flies that are predominantly black in appearance score well. The Stoat's Tail is, therefore, very popular in sizes 8 and 10 or, as an alternative to the more sombre pattern, many Awe fishermen will give a swim to one of the various patterns of Shrimp Fly.

**Access**

Salmon fishing on the Awe is not generally available and certainly not at short notice to the casual visitor. As the river is owned by two syndicates, it also tends to be the rule that their members will, naturally enough, have taken their pick of the best times. Nevertheless, serious inquiries can be made to any of the following:

*Inverawe and Lorn Beat*
Inverawe Fisheries
*Telephone* 08662 262

*Muckairn Beat*
A. R. Nelson
*Telephone* 08662 241

*Barrage Beat*
Bell Ingram's
*Telephone* 0738 21121

## ORCHY

The Orchy flows out of Loch Tulla close to Black Mount and then for a distance of about 10 miles to Loch Awe. I would not be alone in describing Glen Orchy as one of the prettiest glens in the West Highlands. And, besides the scenery, because the Orchy is the major feeder into the loch, and because it provides extensive spawning areas, it is also the most significant part of the system so far as salmon fishing is concerned, though sea-trout are fairly few and far between.

Halfway down the Orchy there is a magnificent waterfall. This has a noticeable effect upon fishing, depending upon whether or not salmon are ascending.

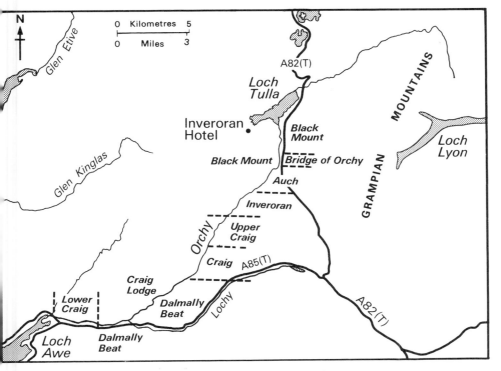

Map 9   *The Beats on the Orchy*

**Season**

11 February to 15 October (best July–September).

**Fish and Fishing**

Since the barrage was raised on the River Awe, that river has been able to show sport earlier in the season. The reason for this is that fish swimming up the Awe, heading eventually through Loch Awe and up to the Orchy, are held up. One man's gain is another man's loss and, obviously, these salmon cannot be in two places at the same time. Therefore, although salmon were historically expected in the Orchy by March and April, the season on the Orchy in modern times does not really get under way until towards the end of May.

Whether it stems from impatience at being held back by the Awe barrage or what is not clear, but the habit of the May fish coming into the Orchy is to run hard through the river's lower beats and on to pools such as the Pulpit and the Gut below the Iron Bridge Falls. There is a tendency, then, for the Orchy to fill from the falls back, with lower beats showing just that little bit later sport than those in the middle.

Salmon are now held back by the falls until the first rains and spate of June, when the salmon pour up towards Loch Tulla. The most productive months, therefore, are July, August and September. Unfortunately, I think, the fishing is continued on into October. I say unfortunately because, by then, there is little if any hope of taking fresh fish and it does seem a pity that the Orchy does not follow the lead set by the Awe in stopping fishing at the end of September.

One other rather contentious issue on the Orchy is the use of spinner and bait in addition to the fly. The indiscriminate use of spinner and bait, particularly where the fly can work so well, is something that is coming in for close scrutiny in the modern age. The fact is that fly fishermen feel the spinner and bait, particularly prawn and shrimp, hurt their own fishing chances. One section of private water is fished virtually fly-only and its effectiveness is adequately illustrated by double-figure catches in a day. I personally would hesitate to suggest that the fly is somehow more sporting than other methods, but there can be little doubt that, for the great majority of fishermen, it is seen as being far and away the most socially considerate.

The Orchy is another of those rivers that prove the effectiveness of quite tiny salmon flies for summer use. Sizes 8 down to 12 double and long-shanked trebles take plenty of fish. Popular patterns include the Stoat, Silver Stoat, Tosh, Sweep, Shrimp, and so on.

If I seem to be thoroughly against the use of anything but the fly on rivers the like of the Orchy, I will readily admit that there are certain pools where, if you hope to catch a fish, you are left with no realistic alternative to the spinner or bait. I am thinking, in this particular instance, of some of the deep, rocky gorges close to falls on the Orchy and some other rivers. The fly purist might say that such areas might be viewed as salmon sanctuaries or as even greater challenges to the fly fisherman's skill. It is really up to the individual to decide which stance he should take. Personally, while I recognize the role of spinner and bait, I plead loudly that they should only be used selectively, rather than indiscriminately, whether on the Orchy or any other river.

## Access

The map on page 63 clearly shows the progression of beats on the Orchy from Loch Tulla down to Loch Awe. Not all beats, it should be noted, let their fishing to the public. Starting at the top:

*Black Mount*
Private water.

*Bridge of Orchy Hotel Beat*
Guests at the hotel have first call on this single-bank beat and rent their fishing at a reduced rate. Contact:

> Bridge of Orchy Hotel
> *Telephone* 08384 208

*Auch Water*
Single bank fished by the tenants of certain self-catering cottages in the area. Contact:

> D. M. MacKinnon & Co
> Station Road
> Oban
> *Telephone* 0631 63014

*Inveroran Hotel Beat*
Details of this single-bank fishing can be obtained from Croggan Crafts (see Dalmally Beat).

*Upper Craig*
For details and terms apply to:

> L. Campbell
> Arichastlich
> Glen Orchy
> Dalmally
> Argyll
> *Telephone* 083 82 282

*Craig Beat*
For details and terms apply to:

> J. K. Miller
> Wooladon Farm
> Lifton
> Devon
> *Telephone* 0566 84 271

*Craig Lodge Beat*
For details and terms of this single-bank fishing apply to Croggan Crafts (see Dalmally Beat) or to:

> C. MacFarlane-Barrow
> Craig Lodge
> Dalmally
> Argyll
> *Telephone* 083 82 216

*Lower Craig*
This again is single-bank fishing. Contacts differ according to whether you wish to take a daily or weekly ticket. For daily tickets apply to Croggan Crafts (see below); for weekly, to:

> West Highland Estates
> 7 Argyll Street
> Oban
> Argyll
> *Telephone* 0631 63617

*Dalmally Beat*
All of the Dalmally beat is single-bank fishing.

That part of the Dalmally beat from the Schoolhouse pool to Catnish footbridge is fished by tenants of self-catering cottages. Details from West Highland Estates (see Lower Craig).

That part of the Dalmally beat from Railway Bridge to Catnish footbridge is handled by Croggan Crafts. As will have already been seen in the details of other Orchy beats, Croggan Crafts handle a number of waters, and are always happy to help the visiting angler. As they say in their own leaflet describing fishing in the area: 'Please give us a call when you are in the area, or phone us for a fishing report. We fish a lot ourselves and meet many fishing folk, so have an idea what is being caught and what fly or lure is best at the time.'

> Croggan Crafts
> Dalmally
> Argyll
> *Telephone* 083 82 201

## ISLE OF MULL

Mull has been described as an angler's paradise. It is certainly one of the most beautiful islands of the Inner Hebrides, with a feeling that is unique, trapped somewhere between isle and mainland. Its coastal waters offer outstanding sea fishing for a great variety of species, and no fewer than eight Scottish records have been set by boats out of Tobermory. The quality of its loch fishing for trout can be quite excellent. But here we are concerned with its salmon and sea-trout, a mixture of river and loch sport that can add up to an almost unique game-fishing experience. In the more specific details of fisheries that follow (described from north to south), it should not be assumed because more details have been given of some waters that those are necessarily the best; it is simply that information about them is more freely available.

### Season

11 February to 31 October (best July–October for salmon, June–October for sea-trout).

### Fish and Fishing

For sea-trout, primarily a question of loch fishing, there is a great tradition on Hebridean waters for fishing fairly bulky palmered-hackled flies. Therefore on Mull we see such favourites as the Black Zulu, the Dark Mackerel, the Bibio, the Soldier Palmer and the

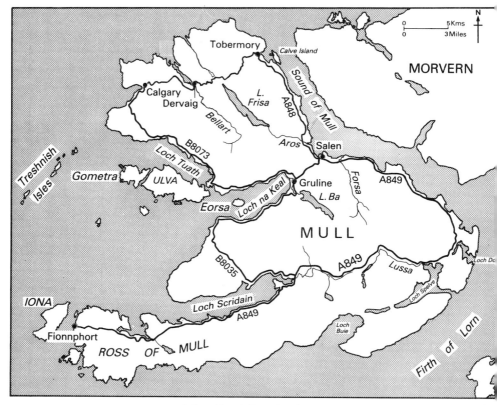

Map 10    *The Isle of Mull*

Black Pennell. You will note that these are all bob flies, to be fished on the top dropper of a cast. Careful working of the bob accounts for a hefty proportion of loch and river sea-trout.

For salmon, on rivers as well as lochs, the use of a dropper should never be discounted when fishing Hebridean and West Highland waters. Flies such as the Black Pennell and the Camasunary Killer on the dropper will take their share of summer salmon and grilse, as well as sea-trout. More traditional flies, mainly for use on the point of the cast, might be chosen from local favourites such as the Hairy Mary, Blue Charm, Thunder and Lightning and the ever popular Stoat's Tail, in either its black- or silver-bodied form to cover the options of dark or bright fly.

As to which rod to use for river fishing, it is little more than personal preference as to whether a single-handed rod of 10 or 11 feet is used, or a double-handed of about 13 feet. None of Mull's rivers is wide, and the accent in casting is very much more on accuracy than sheer range. If the single-handed rod is chosen, then this will obviously double for loch fishing, as well as covering sea-trout needs.

Note that the best time for sea-trout is from June right through into October. Those who have experienced catching fresh-run Mull sea-trout in October – well protected against the cold and fortified by the distant sound of the roaring stags at the rut, and maybe a dram or two – say that this late-season sea-trouting is one of the unforgettable game-fishing experiences.

## LOCH TORR

The northernmost loch on Mull was purpose-built for fishing in 1899. Fishing is by fly only, and there are two boats to be had on the loch. It should, however, be pointed out that Torr has built its reputation very largely on its stock of wild brown trout and stocked rainbows. Sea-trout and, to an even greater extent, salmon are seen more as an extra attraction taken in the course of trout fishing. However, if you want to try specifically for sea-trout on Torr, then the best time to try is September.

### Permit

Tackle and Books in Tobermory (*telephone* 0688 2336).

## RIVER BELLART

Although it produces salmon, the Bellart is best known for its sea-trout. Large shoals of finnock, fairly small sea-trout, run the river at any time from May onwards, particularly on spring tides and when the river rises in spate, after which it is possible to hook a dozen fish in a day. On a personal note, however, I would add that you should really not take any more finnock than you can eat for breakfast as these are immature fish that will, if left, return as bigger fish at a later date.

### Permit

Tackle and Books, as above.

*Playing a Hebridean sea-trout: Loch Ba, Mull*

## LOCH FRISA

When we fished Loch Frisa, I hooked two salmon but I was told that this was something of an achievement because, while salmon and sea-trout are often seen in the loch, they are rarely caught. Frisa's reputation is for excellent trout fishing but only occasional encounters with migratory fish. If you want to try, remember that this loch, the largest on Mull, is over 11 miles in circumference, so book a boat! Either from Tackle and Books or the Forestry Commission, at Aros (*telephone* 06803 346).

## RIVER AROS

This river is less than 5 miles long and yet it is fed by innumerable burns and, on its day, can yield excellent sport. One of the tributaries, the Ledmore river, flows out of Loch Frisa.

Salmon and grilse run the Aros at any time during the summer months from late June to August, depending, as you would expect, on sufficiently high water levels after rain to draw them up from the salt. However, the run can be delayed even until October if the Aros's headwaters experience a summer drought.

The Aros also enjoys good runs of sea-trout. These occur from May onwards, though some fishermen would hedge their bets and hope for rain in late June to set the fish running.

No description of the Aros would be complete without an account of the heaviest rod-caught salmon ever taken on Mull. It was on the morning of 30 August 1911 that James Greenhill's worm was sucked in by a big fish. It was six hours later before John MacColl, the gillie, was able to gaff out the 45-lb cock salmon. One of the reasons for this prolonged fight was, no doubt, Mr Greenhill's concern over his gut cast, which, it is said, had a breaking strain of less than 12 lb. Even so, this seems an inordinately long time. But what a magnificent salmon to catch in an area where virtually any salmon in double figures is a subject of note!

Fishing permission from Captain D. Scott at Glenaros (*telephone* 06803 337).

## RIVER BA

This river, which runs out of Loch Ba, is only 2½ miles long. Where it enters the sea at Killiechronan by Loch na Keal there is a big pool; in fact it is enormous by Hebridean standards. In the old days when this pool was netted it is said that the numbers of salmon taken would often fill a cart. Certainly, when a spring tide brings salmon in but there is insufficient water in the river for them to run any higher, literally dozens of salmon will be seen in this stretch. There will also be sea-trout aplenty, including large ones, from as early as April. Mullet are also seen swarming into the river during June and July, which may cause frustration to an inexperienced angler who keeps casting his fly over them in the belief that they are sea-trout. Such tactics rarely work on mullet! Normally, the main runs of salmon and sea-trout run the river from June to October. The fishing on this river, as on the loch, is only occasionally available, though the public have more chance of fishing the sea pools. In either case, inquiries should be made to Killiechronan Estates (*telephone* 06803 438).

## LOCH BA

Loch Ba, also let by the Killiechronan Estates, is described as a very good loch for salmon and big sea-trout. In fact, it has produced sea-trout of almost 20 lb, and double-figure fish have not been uncommon in the past. A fair proportion of these big sea-trout are taken on the dap, though individual fishermen might argue that a cleverly worked bob fly fished in the traditional loch style can work just as well, if not better. There is something that sea-trout find very provocative in a big, heavily hackled fly on the wavetops, be it a dap or a bob. The other popular method on Loch Ba, besides the dap and wet fly, is to spin or troll with a Toby spoon.

## RIVER FORSA

This is widely regarded as one of the best salmon rivers on Mull. It has some 40 holding pools, which allows it to be divided into six beats. These are rotated so that the angler has the chance of fishing the entire river.

The Forsa is Mull's longest salmon river, flowing for 10 miles. It fishes best in a spate, and from July to October. Many fish are taken on the worm or by spinning, but that is not to say that it does not yield equally good sport to the fly. An occasional salmon of close to 20 lb may be taken but, as is expected on western rivers, island and mainland, the average weight is less than 10 lb. No problem there, however, and these grilse-sized fish give tremendous sport on reasonably sensitive tackle.

Incidentally, the Forsa, like so many spate rivers of the islands, rises and falls very quickly in times of spate. I recall that one evening it was raining during dinner and when we went to bed, but the night-time spate had virtually fallen away by breakfast. Taking times on rivers such as this are often measured in hours rather than days, and being in the right place at the right time becomes the angler's preoccupation.

### Access

Permits, when available, can be obtained from a number of sources: Glenforsa Hotel (*telephone* 06803 377); Tackle and Books (0688 2336); and Mull Travel and Crafts (06802 487).

## RIVER LUSSA

The Lussa flows out of Loch Sguabain, and fish can ascend only during spates. It is a beautiful little river of holding pools and runs punctuated with miniature falls. There is, however, one rather larger waterfall at Tor Ness, some 3½ miles up from the sea. Salmon may tarry here for a while, but then surmount the falls and travel on upstream. However, it is noted that the larger class of salmon, including a 24-pounder in 1946 and a 34-pounder back in the 1920s, are caught at or below Tor Ness.

The main runs of salmon are expected in June and July, and good runs of sea-trout enter the Lussa in late May and June.

The Forestry Commission controls 1½ miles of the river (*telephone* 06803 346).

## LOCH SGUABAIN

Those boat fishermen who appreciate a brisk breeze to aid their drift may be interested to note that the nearest English translation of the Gaelic *Sguabain* is 'windswept'. It is said that Sguabain's surface is invariably ruffled by wind to create excellent drifting conditions.

One characteristic of the loch is dense weed in certain parts. There are two possible solutions. Either fly the dap to settle the big fly on top of the weed or, preferably, between it; or fish a single wet fly and accept the inevitable need, every so often, to clear the hook of weed. The reward can be a salmon or an excellent sea-trout, but mind how you play it in the vicinity of those weeds.

It is boat fishing only on Loch Sguabain, and permission can be obtained from Glenforsa Hotel, Aros (*telephone* 06803 377); Mull Travel, Craignure (06802 487); Tackle and Books, Tobermory (0688 2336); and J. McKeand, Scoor, Fionnphort (06817 297).

## RIVER COLADOIR

The Coladoir flows from Loch Fuaron and offers 4 miles of pools and glides. There are falls getting up towards the loch, but fish do not seem to have any problem in ascending them.

Dependent upon ever-important rainfall to raise the water levels in the river, fish will run the Coladoir from the end of June through until October. July can be a very good month, given rain. It is, perhaps, for its sea-trout that the river is best known.

Permission to fish the Coladoir should be sought from Sandie Peddie at Rossal (*telephone* 06814 210).

## LOCH ASSAPOL

This loch lies towards the south-west tip of Mull. It is a generally shallow loch with occasional deep holes. Much of Assapol's reputation has been built on its brown-trout fishing, with some very big ferox specimens making the news, usually towards the end of the season. One novice angler caught his first ever trout in Loch Assapol on a Devon minnow in a couple of feet of water. It weighed a feather over 7½ lb.

There are runs of sea-trout coming up into the loch from May onwards, as well as some salmon and grilse.

Permits are available from J. McKeand, Scoor House, Fionnphort (*telephone* 06817 297); Argyll Arms Hotel, Bunessan (06817 240); and W. L. Rosier, Assapol House (06817 258).

# 4 Fort William to Skye

## NEVIS

The Nevis is not really one of those rivers that you would plan to fish months ahead, but it can, on its day, yield good sport with sea-trout and, to a lesser extent, grilse and salmon. Surely, however, this is typical of so many spate streams to be found in the Western Highlands and Islands. They are what we might choose to call opportunists' rivers. In the right spot and, above all, at the right time, you may have a happy and productive time, but if your visit does not coincide with suitable water heights – well, as they say, you may as well stay at home and fish in a bucket!

So that is how I think of the Nevis, a merry little stream that ran past my office when I worked for a time in Fort William. I had only to open my window to hear whether it was likely to produce the goods. A merry, gurgling song did little to raise my spirits. It took a thunderous roar to get me looking at my watch and wondering how soon I could slip away. For the Nevis is in the classic form of spate river, fishing really well only as it falls and clears. The main runs of migratory fish are expected from late June to early August.

The river runs down Glen Nevis, skirting round Ben Nevis, the highest mountain in Britain. As you can imagine, the Nevis therefore scores top marks for scenic backdrop. The fishing is normally by fly only but, during a spate, the worm is permitted and can be very productive. Spinning is prohibited at all times.

## Season

11 February to 31 October.

## Access

The Nevis is controlled by the Fort William Angling Club. Day tickets, which are not issued until 9 a.m. on the required day, are obtainable from:

> Rod & Gun Shop
> The High Street
> Fort William
> *Telephone* 0397 2656

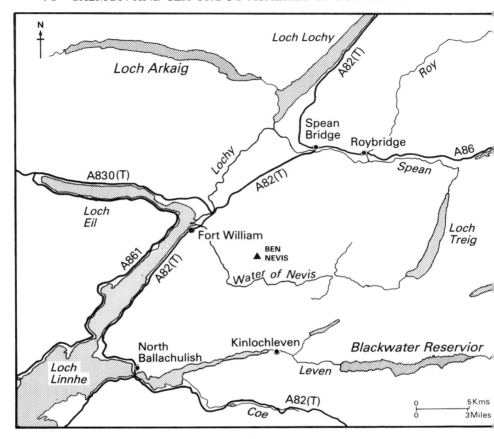

Map 11   *Fort William area*

## LOCHY

The Lochy is the largest and most prolific salmon river in the Fort William area. Its major tributaries are the Spean and the Roy.

The River Lochy flows from Loch Lochy. This is the most western loch of the system which makes up the Caledonian Canal, running along the line of the Great Fault between Fort William on the west coast and Inverness on the east. Mucomir power station creates a barrage to dam the lower end of Loch Lochy and, therefore, the flow in the river is under this control. Deep-wading anglers should always bear this point in mind, and keep a weather eye open for a fast rise in water levels when the power station starts to generate. Other than this, the Lochy is a grand river to wade and fish, though some of its larger pools, on the private waters, are perhaps best fished from a boat.

It is worth mentioning the scenery. Ben Nevis, the highest mountain in Britain, stands just to the east and adds the finishing touch to what is truly magnificent Highland scenery. The river sweeps over fine gravel beds and past rocky shores to provide outstanding water for fishing the fly. This part of the West Highlands is noted for its Norwegian fjord-like sea lochs. A truly grand setting for a salmon fishing holiday!

## Season

11 February to 31 October.

## Fishing

Most of the Lochy fishing is let privately through the River Lochy Association. There is, however, a public stretch. This is Beat 7, inquiries for which should be made to the Rod and Gun Shop in Fort William. This is an excellent stretch of water – even if it receives a share of adverse publicity concerning the activities of those who do not mind whether their salmon are hooked in the mouth, flank or back. It yields in the region of 400 to 500 migratory fish each season. Beat 7 stretches from tidal waters up to about a mile upstream of Fort William. Spinning is allowed only on a limited section, and then only when the water is above a certain height.

## Fish

The Lochy season gets under way in April and May, though what fish there are at this time of the year are not numerous. The main runs and catches occur from the end of May through to early August. After that, few fresh salmon enter the river, and the resident stock are becoming stale and coloured.

Although this is very much a summer spate river with a good head of grilse and sea-trout, the Lochy is also capable of producing larger salmon. Each season should see a number of salmon in the 20–25-lb class and, just occasionally, a 30-pounder is reported.

## Tackle and Technique

The Lochy is an excellent river for fly fishing. Many patterns of flies have proved their worth but local favourites for summer use would include the Stoat's Tail, both black- and silver-bodied, the Blue Charm in hair- and feather-winged versions, Hairy Mary,

Jeannie and one of the ever popular patterns of Shrimp Fly – all carried in sizes 6–12 on doubles or long-shanked Drury-type trebles.

A tail race from the aluminium smelting plant enters the Lochy on the public stretch, Beat 7, and this can affect tackle choice. The water is fed from a high loch at low temperature, and the flow can be fierce. Therefore, a large tube such as a Willie Gunn or Garry Dog may be used on a sinking line. This is not an invitation to sniggle, but a suggestion as to how best to fish the strong tail race.

Sea-trout fishing comes into its own with the fading light of dusk and, being so close to tidal waters, can be quite spectacular for those prepared to set aside thoughts of salmon.

Traditional sea-trout patterns work well on the Lochy, with a number of fishermen choosing a double for the point and a bushy palmered fly on the dropper. You would not go far wrong if making a choice from established favourites such as the Peter Ross, Black Pennell, Cinnamon and Gold, Dark Mackerel, Dunkeld, Invicta, or the deadly Teal, Blue and Silver. Tandem patterns have their devotees but standard hooks, sizes 8 and 10, are very successful.

## Access

*Public Stretch*

> Rod and Gun Shop
> High Street
> Fort William
> *Telephone* 0397 2656

*Private Water*
Access is strictly limited, with waiting lists, but serious inquiries can be made to:

> J. C. Parry
> The Old Rectory
> Allington
> Grantham
> Lincolnshire

## LOCH LOCHY

The fishing on Loch Lochy is free, with no permit being required. Therefore, as you would expect, while this loch can provide good sport with brown trout, salmon and sea-trout tend to be few and far between. Can be fished with fly or spinner, and boats can be hired from:

> Mrs Duck
> Poplar Cottage
> Bunarkaig
> *Telephone* 0397 81

## SPEAN

The Spean, and Spean Bridge in particular, will always be associated in many minds with the commandos and their memorial, for it was in this area during the Second World War that they trained. In other, perhaps younger, minds, the Spean is associated with good salmon sport in a spectacular setting.

The headwaters and lochs that used to feed the Spean were dammed or redirected to provide power to the British Aluminium

*Sea-trout fishing in tidal water is often available if you seek permission from the riparian owner. But remember to wash off the corrosive salt water and don't rest reels in the sand!*

Company in Fort William. With no compensation flow, the Spean might have been virtually destroyed as a salmon river. However, it has one major tributary. This is the Roy, which is considered below. In order for the Spean to fish well nowadays, the Roy must rise in spate. This water, flowing into the Spean, brings up its water levels. In fact, the situation is such that most authorities are agreed that those salmon caught in the Spean are not really Spean fish at all but ones heading for the Roy to spawn. Nevertheless, while these fish are in the Spean they can provide excellent sport.

**Season**

11 February to 31 October (best July–September).

**Fish and Fishing**

The Spean has gained something of a reputation for producing big fish. One that immediately springs to mind is a salmon of 37 lb caught in 1976. This, allied to the steep and rocky nature of the river (which, incidentally, make it unsuitable for the unsteady or infirm), means that you should not consider fishing too light. It takes good strong nylon to land a hefty fish, particularly where the cast may be abraded on rocks. As the Spean fishes best on the heels of a spate, 15 lb bs nylon should perhaps be viewed as an absolute minimum when fishing the locally favoured tube flies.

Bait fishing is banned and spinning is far and away the favoured method of fishing the Spean at high water times. I would tend to disregard virtually every other lure in favour of a Toby spoon for this work. The Toby has been described as one of the greatest attractors of salmon and, in strong, streamy water, there is nothing quite like it. Silver or gold seem the most popular colours and you should not be worried about fishing one of the longer sizes such as the 18-gram. A stiffish rod of about 9 feet and a fixed-spool reel complete the outfit.

**Access**

There are a number of beats on the Spean. Some are under the control of angling clubs, others are private, and local hotels such as the Spean Bridge may be able to arrange fishing. The best source of advice on access to the Spean, and most waters in the district, is the Rod and Gun Shop in Fort William. Certainly, they control the fishing on Beat A, on which two rods are allowed each day. Like the Nevis, and the stretch they control on the Lochy, the rule is that permits are not issued till 9 a.m. on the day required. Believe me, if the fishing conditions are good, do not bother turning up at the shop door at 9 a.m. The fact of the matter is that you will have to join the back of what might be a fairly long queue, and it's first come, first served, and devil take the hindmost!

Rod and Gun Shop
The High Street
Fort William
*Telephone* 0397 2656

## ROY

The Roy flows into the Spean about 4 miles upstream of Spean Bridge. In an area where so many waters have suffered to some extent at the hands of man, it is almost a relief to find that here is one little spate river that has been left in its natural state. Spates in the Roy bring up the Spean as well, and draw migratory fish into both rivers. Virtually all fish that run the Spean are ultimately bound for the Roy. There is no loch to act as a reserve of water on the headstreams of the Roy and, therefore, it is heavily dependent on recent rain so far as fishing chances are concerned.

Unlike the Spean, where the rule is fly or spinner only, on the Roy the worm is permitted. Indeed, this method is particularly suited to the nature of the Roy and there can be little doubt that the worm is the most productive choice.

### Season

11 February to 31 October (best July–September).

### Access

Permits to fish the Roy are available from either of two hotels, Roy Bridge Hotel (*telephone* 0397 81 236) and Stronlossit Hotel (*telephone* 0397 81 253).

## ALINE

It may seem strange that the Aline is the only fishery in Ardgour and Morven to merit inclusion but the fact of the matter is that virtually all other waters in this area are strictly preserved and therefore outside the scope of this book.

The Aline is a good little river which drains into the sea on the southern shores of the Morven peninsula, looking straight across at Mull. Indeed, there is a ferry from Lochaline to Fishnish.

The river is about 3 miles long, and is part of an interesting water system. The Aline flows out of Loch Arienas and, just a short distance below the loch, is joined by two tributaries, which themselves unite about 100 yards before flowing into the Aline. The two tributaries flow down from their respective glens, the Black Glen and the White Glen – or, if you have the Gaelic, Gleann Dubh and Gleann Geal. What is so fascinating about this system is that when the tributaries rise in spate there comes a point where the water in the Aline above the confluence actually starts to flow back on itself to fill Loch Arienas with a reserve of water that acts as nature's store, and maintains the Aline at a fishing height for a prolonged period. A clever little ruse, and perfectly natural.

What is also very clever, but entirely man-made, is a dam set below the waterfalls in the White Glen. The effect is to deepen the falls pool, and thus reduce the height that fish have to leap in order to ascend the falls.

The Aline system fishes well from June onwards, and is divided into three beats, each of which accommodates three rods, and which rotate. Other beats are White Glen, fished for salmon and sea-trout from June to October but only in spate conditions; Loch Arienas, where boats and outboards are available for hire to pursue its salmon and sea-trout; and Loch Tearnait, a large hill loch where a boat is also provided.

**Season**

11 February to 31 October (best June–mid-October).

**Access**

All this fishing, as well as a number of other hill lochs which can fish well for trout, is controlled by Ardtornish Estate, which also has the fishing on the Rannoch, a very close neighbour to the Aline. Fishing is normally let in association with holiday cottages. For details contact:

Ardtornish Estate Office
Morvern
by Oban
*Telephone* 096 784 288

# SHIEL

The Shiel is one of those systems of short river and long loch that we associate so strongly with the Western Highlands, a river of only 3 miles below an 18-mile-long loch – a loch which, for its length, is perhaps the narrowest in Scotland, with a definitely fjord-like appearance above Polloch. This top end of the loch, with the mountains dropping straight down into it, virtually without a shore in parts, is very deep in places. It grows shallower at the lower end, towards the outflow of the river.

Between the loch and the river's mouth in saltwater Loch Moidart there is very little fall. Indeed, the fall is barely more than 20 feet over the river's 3-mile length. This tends towards a slow, sluggish flow over a bed of mud and fine gravel brought down from the loch. Weed growth can, at times, be quite heavy in certain stretches. All this despite the fact that the river, in its middle section, flows through what amounts to a rocky gorge. Rocky gorge is perhaps the wrong description. As a boy, when fishing the loch, I would go down to the river in the evenings, and, with its deep but slow holding pools, this 'gorge' had more the feel of a tranquil oriental water garden. The hand of man is very much in evidence on the river. Besides the carefully tended fishing stages from which the angler casts and the soft, fertile meadowland through which the river flows, with rhododendrons and azalias in bloom, there are man-made groynes placed in an attempt to harness the water flow.

## Season

11 February to 31 October (best June–September).

## Fish and Fishing

### The River
Although the system can enjoy excellent runs of summer salmon and grilse, it is primarily with sea-trout that I associate the Shiel. Due to the slow nature of the river, in daylight it will fish well only at times of high water or when there is a stiff breeze to ruffle the water on the long flats. And so, at other times, the Shiel fisherman waits patiently for the short summer nights to hide his approach. But then what sport this short river can produce! Sure, the bags may never again be so heavy as back in the fish-rich sixties, but the quality of sea-trout sport remains very good and a grilse or summer

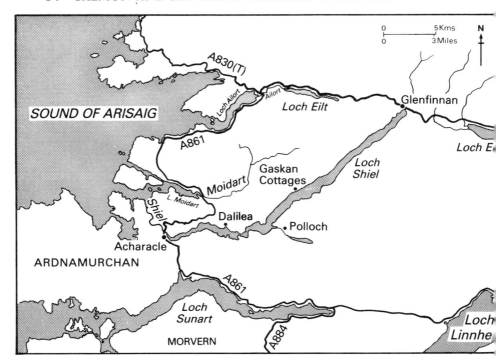

Map 12    *Rivers Shiel, Modiart, Ailort and Loch Eilt*

salmon taken in the fading light of dusk or the first glow of dawn adds to the whole pleasure of the thing.

For this class of through-the-night fishing, a rod of 10 to 11 feet seems the perfect solution. The floating line is by far the most pleasant way to fish though, after the initial activity of the dusk rise, it can pay to change to a sinker. I am not sure, but I do not think that the modern, longer, larger class of sea-trout flies have made much of an impact on Highland waters. Sizes 8 and 10 are much more the thing, with possibly a smallish demon, terror-type lure to use in the darkest part of the night, if the fish are reluctant to move to the small fly. It is my experience, however, that they may be just as likely to snatch at a tiny size 12 double or a worm fly inched back on the sinking line. It does not pay to become too stereotyped in our approach to river sea-trout and on the Shiel, as elsewhere, we should at least be prepared to ring the changes. But it does little harm to make a start with floating line and size 8 traditional favourites such as the Peter Ross or Dunkeld on the point, and a Wickham's or Dark Mackerel on a dropper.

## The Loch

I do not think it unfair to suggest that on Loch Shiel wet-fly fishing and dapping spells sport with sea-trout but, for salmon, most regulars rely extensively on trolling, with an 18-gram copper Toby serving as well as anything. Trolling is fully described in the section on Loch Lomond (pages 44–5).

Traditional wet-fly fishing techniques tend to rely heavily on a stiff breeze to set a rolling wave on the surface of the loch. Modern trout fishermen might see sea-trout technique as a combination of long- and short-lining. The flies are cast out ahead of the drifting boat and retrieved in long steady pulls, far quicker than would normally be productive for trout. Then, while the pulls are continued, the long rod is raised, causing the top dropper or bob fly to come scuttering up to the surface – a deadly moment in terms of attracting sea-trout.

When choosing a sea-trout fly for the bob position, on the Shiel or anywhere else come to that, remember that the sea-trout has a preference for deep-water lies, certainly deeper than those we associate with salmon. It is never safe to be dogmatic on such matters but, as a general rule, look for sea-trout in depths from 6 up to 20 feet. Do not be frightened, therefore, to go for a big, heavily hackled bob fly, say a size 6 Soldier Palmer, to create sufficient surface disturbance to bring up a fish. And fish it fast. Again, no hard and fast rules but, in the general way of things, sea-trout are attracted to flies that would be considered as far too speedy for either brown trout or salmon.

This attraction of surface disturbance is taken to its logical conclusion in dapping. An extremely long rod and a light floss line carry a big fly out on the breeze to settle gently and play on the waves, dancing, tripping and bobbing until up comes a sea-trout. Dapping, done with thought and concentrated effort, can be an excellent technique for taking sea-trout. It is described in depth in the section on Loch Maree (page 97).

## Access

Access to the River Shiel is strictly limited. It helps to know 'the friend of a friend'. The fishing on the north bank is owned by Dorlin Estate and the south bank is controlled by a syndicate.

Access to Loch Shiel is far more straightforward. The choice that has to be made, in the first place, is whether to fish the eastern, top end or the bottom, western end. The fact is that while access to the top end at Glenfinnan is easy, as it is at the Acharachle end, there is no access except by boat to the middle. The Black Rocks, roughly midway between Acharachle and Glenfinnan, offer fine sea-trout fishing on their day, in utterly remote circumstances, but 9 miles there and then back again in the evening make them the subject of a special trip, whichever end you approach them from.

*Eastern End*
Trolling is the reliable method at the start of the season in May, but then the fly really comes into its own in late June and through to September, when the sea-trout are at their most plentiful. Those who fish this top end may argue that the sea-trout running up Loch Shiel do not stop in the loch until they are within sight of the Glenfinnan Monument, which commemorates the landing of Prince Charles Edward Stuart and the rising of the clans for the Forty-Five. Whether or not Shiel sea-trout hold such Jacobite loyalties, the top end of the loch can certainly show some excellent sport. The dap is particularly effective later in the season. Contact:

> Stage House Inn
> Glenfinnan
> *Telephone* 0397 83 246

> Glenfinnan House Hotel
> Glenfinnan
> *Telephone* 0397 83 235

*Western End*
Permission to fish Loch Shiel from the western, seaward end is available from a number of sources. Incidentally, this permission will include the use of a boat and outboard because, besides its sheer size, no bank fishing is allowed anywhere on Loch Shiel, top or bottom. Contact Loch Shiel Hotel (*telephone* 096785 253), Clanranald Hotel (*telephone* 098 785 662), or D. Macaulay, Dalilea Farm, Acharachle, who has six boats and accommodation (*telephone* 096785 253).

## AILORT AND LOCH EILT

The Ailort is a small river which drains Loch Eilt and lies on the Road to the Isles a few miles beyond Glenfinnan. Although the road runs along its northern shore, and the railway along the south, it maintains an idyllic setting in some fine, rugged West Highland scenery.

## Season

11 February to 31 October (best June–September).

## Fish and Fishing

In times past Loch Eilt had a reputation for producing some of the best sea-trout fishing of any loch in Britain. Nowadays, as on virtually all western waters, this fishery has suffered in terms both of quality and of quantity. An interesting experiment has been tried, however, with the co-operation of the local salmon farm. Sea-trout have been reared in Loch Eilt, then taken down to cages in saltwater Loch Ailort. Following spates, these fish were released and ran up the Ailort and back into the loch.

Both river and loch are maintained as fly-only waters. The dap is also allowed, and is a very popular method for rising the larger class of sea-trout during August and September. September is generally the best month for salmon from both river and loch.

## Access

Full details and permission to fish both river and loch can be had from:

> Lochailort Inn
> Lochailort
> *Telephone* 06877 208

## CROE

The Croe, a small spate river in Kintail, is well worth looking at. A fly-only river, it is owned by the National Trust for Scotland. It is a small spate river, heavily dependent upon rain to bring it into best form, but it yields a surprisingly good number of salmon, grilse and sea-trout.

The Croe has no falls and is far from being steep. Indeed, it tends if anything towards deep, slow pools and fairly sluggish stretches. It is only 4 miles long on its course down Gleann Lichd and into the sea. Due perhaps to the protection of the National Trust, the Croe remains in its natural state, unsullied by the hand of man the developer.

## Season

11 February to 31 October (best July–September).

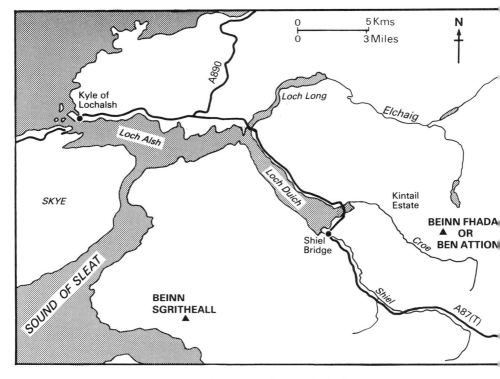

Map 13    *Rivers Croe and Shiel*

## Fish and Fishing

Perhaps the most noticeable feature of the Croe from the fishing
point of view is that, except in times of high spate, the river runs
virtually gin clear. It is fairly easy to see the salmon lying in the
pools. The only problem, of course, is that if the fisherman can see
the fish the fish can see the fisherman! A stealthy reconnaissance is
recommended, then a sensitive approach, as if one were stalking
deer on the high hills. Finally, you must be prepared to fish fairly
light and with delicacy. As you might expect, a breeze to ruffle the
surface is a help in such conditions and even then a small fly is all
that is required: something like a Hairy Mary, Stoat or Tosh on a
10 or 12 double or long-shanked treble can work the magic. And
remember, as you may well be lucky enough to see the fish actually
moving to your fly, never strike until you feel the fish's weight on
the rod – 'better to delay than snatch it away'.

Salmon may well be seen in the Croe as early as April or May, but sport is usually at its best in the period from July to September. July should also see the first runs of sea-trout. The average weight of these sea-trout will be in the region of 2 lb, though they have been caught up to 6 lb, which, incidentally, is about the average weight of salmon and grilse caught on the Croe, with the record being set by a marvellous fish of 19 lb. The fishing tends to be fading a bit in October, although it is still possible to catch fresh salmon right up to season's close at the end of October.

## Access

Permission to fish the Croe is handled by the National Trust's agent at Morvich Farm. Four rods are allowed, but be warned that due to the popularity of this exceptional little spate river vacancies tend to be few and far between. Contact:

Morvich Farm
by Kyle of Lochalsh
*Telephone* 059 981 219

## SHIEL

Close to the Croe, just down the coast, is the Shiel of Glenshiel. Like the Croe, it is a small spate river which can run gin clear. Tactics for the Shiel are very similar to those for the Croe. What the Shiel has that the Croe lacks is a small loch on its course, which acts as a big holding pool to running salmon and sea-trout. Given the essential rain to create a spate and bring fish up off the tide, the water fishes well from the end of May through to September, with July and August normally proving the peak months. A boat is available in order to fish the loch.

## Access

Contact:

Mrs Campbell
Shiel House
Glenshiel
*Telephone* 059 981 282

*Playing a sea-trout on the sea pool, River Sheil*

## ISLE OF SKYE

I hope I will be forgiven for saying that while Skye is undoubtedly one of the most picturesque and attractive of the Western Isles it is rather lacking in terms of salmon fishing. It is one of those venues that I would describe as being best suited to the person whose priorities are first a holiday, second a fishing holiday and, third, a salmon–fishing holiday. The fact of the matter is that, while Skye has a number of small spate streams, they will only fish well after rain, and for a fairly short time even then. But this will not deter the fisherman who is prepared to accept these things and while away the drought times with trout or sea fishing, or just lazing on a beach or enjoying the scenery. Do not get me wrong – the streams can fish well, but in their own time, and guarantees can never be offered on any river, let alone a small spate stream.

Added to that, some of the best potential for salmon fishing on Skye is kept a strictly private affair, although a number of hotels are able to offer fishing. The best of the salmon rivers on the island are the Drynoch, Kilmartin, Snizort and Varagill, I have been told. The fish that run up these rivers are seldom large, being better viewed as grilse.

Perhaps the greatest problem facing the salmon rivers of Skye comes from poaching. It has been described as a local cottage industry! Fish entering the rivers on a spate become trapped in small pools as the water falls, after which . . . well, there is just too much water to watch it all.

But, despite all this, Skye salmon and sea-trout are there to be caught on rod and line, given the right conditions.

## Access

So far as I have been able to establish, the Varragill and Drynoch rivers are maintained strictly private. As to the others, it is easiest to list the hotels that have fishing.

Dunvegan Hotel at Dunvegan can offer salmon and sea-trout fishing on rivers Hinnisdale, Mamara and Osdale. *Telephone* 047 022 202.

Skeabost Hotel at Skeabost has 8 miles of the Snizort, one of the better Skye rivers, for the use of their guests. *Telephone* 047 032 202.

Ullinish Lodge Hotel at Struan can also offer salmon and sea-trout on the Snizort, and they have the whole of the Ose, also known as the Ullinish. The Ullinish is one of those rivers with a reputation for becoming particularly peaty at times. *Telephone* 047 072 214.

Besides these hotels, the fishing on several rivers in the northern part of Skye is controlled by the Portree Angling Association, Masonic Buildings, Portree, Isle of Skye.

# 5   The North-West

## AN INTRODUCTION TO THE NORTH-WEST

I should not even try to describe the lands and waters of the north-west Highlands – Scottish dawns and Highland suns over some of the earth's most magnificent scenery, the endless Atlantic sky, the cry of moor fowl and the scent of peat and crushed myrtle, soft Gaelic voices on a distant shore – oh, you could write a dozen books just describing the feel of the place, and still not get it right. The place and the people, the birds, the deer and other creatures of hill, forest and glen and, above all perhaps for us fishermen, the fish and fishing. But this is intended as a book of fact, not feeling, so let us be on with the job in hand.

### Tackle and Techniques

In many cases, where describing the individual rivers and lochs of this area, I shall make specific mention of appropriate tackle and techniques. It can be said, however, that there is a general theme to the thing. With a few notable exceptions, most of the rivers can be fished in either wellington boots or, at most, thigh waders. Indeed, some of the rivers such as the Kirkaig are, perhaps, best approached in climbing boots!

You will understand from that that the rivers of the north-west tend to be on the small side. They are waters where the accent is firmly on casting accuracy, and delicacy when the water is low, rather than casting range. With each returning visit you get to know your chosen river that little bit better, and come to expect a fish to be lying just at the cheek of the white stone at the head of this or that pool. And you will learn how your fly must be presented, hovering and tantalizing, in order to tempt the fish to take. So here is a land where there is little if any need for a double-handed rod of more than 14 feet, even in high water. It is also a traditional land, and therefore we are not surprised to discover rivers where the recommended patterns of flies include the old, classic favourites such as the Yellow Torrish, Thunder and Lightning and Mar Lodge, even tied on big single hooks up to 6/0 for use in high water, as well as the modernists' tubes and Waddingtons, small doubles and long-shanked trebles, which fit the bill, most of the time. And it is a land where we experience combined summer operations, perhaps fishing a Silver Stoat tube on the point and something like a Camasunary Killer on the dropper off a floating line on an 11-foot single-handed rod, never really knowing if the next take will come from a plump little sea-trout, a game little grilse, or a rod-bending, reel-screeching salmon.

And so, travelling north from the Kyle of Lochalsh, the first river we come to is the Applecross.

## APPLECROSS

The principal source of this Wester Ross spate river is on Beinn Bhan. From there, it is a 10-mile journey to the sea at the village of Applecross. Three lochs on the river's headwaters have a significant effect on the river's fishing potential by tending to maintain water heights following a spate.

A great deal of work has been undertaken not only to improve the fishing on this splendidly wild spate river, by increasing the holding potential of many of its pools, but also in improving the access. Before the roads leading to Applecross were improved the area was certainly very remote.

### Season

11 February to 31 October (best June–September).

### Fish and Fishing

The Applecross can be regarded as a typical spate river, being reliant on rain to create spates to bring in fish off the tide and create favourable fishing conditions. Major runs of salmon and sea-trout are to be expected, given the right conditions, from June onwards. Salmon are not large on the Applecross, running to an average of about 7–8 lb, and there will perhaps be 100 caught each season. But every so often a 20-pounder is taken. The class of sea-trout taken on the river is traditionally high, with weights ranging from 1 lb up to as much as 8 lb, though it has to be said that sea-trout do not figure in the bag as often as salmon.

### Access

For further details and permission to fish the Applecross, telephone Applecross Estate Office, 05204 209.

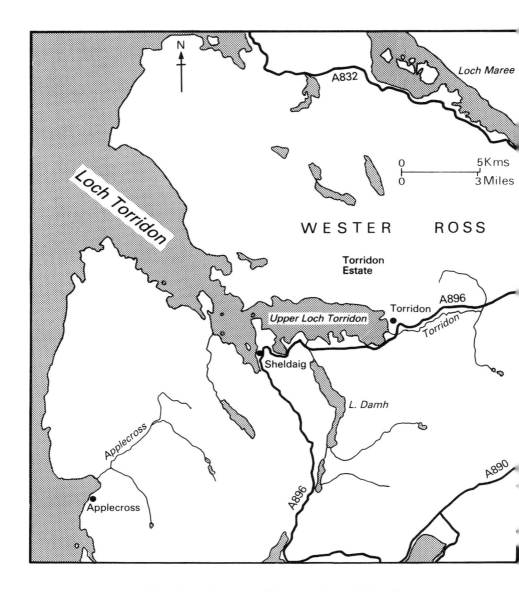

Map 14    *Rivers Applecross, Balgy and Torridon*

## BALGY

The Balgy is a short river, barely more than a mile in length, which flows out of Loch Damph and into the sea not far from the village of Torridon. In that, it is typical of a number of West Highland systems – a short river below a long, narrow loch.

In such a short distance, it is surprising that the Balgy offers such a variety in character. Just below the loch there is a steep gorge and the Falls of Balgy. Below this, however, the river tends towards the sluggish and meandering. Then, finally, for what is left of its short journey to the salt, the Balgy quickens and straightens its flow over a series of small falls and rapids.

### Season

11 February to 31 October (best June–September).

### Fish and Fishing

Given decent water levels, the Balgy can fish very well for salmon, grilse and sea-trout from July through to September, and there may be fish running in June.

Besides the good river fishing, excellent sport can be had with sea-trout on Loch Damph – though, of course, with West Highland sea-trout fortunes being what they are, it is always wise to check to see what is happening and when. If the sea-trout are there, dapping is the popular and productive method for pursuing them. The wet fly also works well.

### Access

The Balgy is jointly owned and fished by two estates. Probably the best option in seeking details and access is to contact:

> Loch Torridon Hotel
> Torridon
> Wester Ross
> *Telephone* 044 507 242

## TORRIDON

This is another small spate river which, like its neighbour the Balgy, can yield sport after rain and spate – but not, it has to be said, in the same quantities as the Balgy. Season and best times are as for the Balgy.

The river has its source in Lochan an Iasgaich, which can produce salmon and sea-trout.

## Access

Permission to fish the Torridon can be sought either from the Loch Torridon Hotel (*telephone* 044 587 242) or from the post office in Torridon village.

## BADACHRO

The Badachro is a short river which runs into the sea close to the village of Gairloch. It is a spate stream, enjoying sport with salmon and grilse after a spate. Perhaps surprisingly, it is reported that sea-trout do not run this river. There is a loch on the river system, Loch Badachro, off which about half of the annual catch of 30–40 salmon are taken on standard tackle and tactics for the region.

## Season

11 February to 31 October (best July–October).

## Access

The Badachro is owned by Gairloch Estate but the fishing is handled by Shieldaig Lodge Hotel, for their guests and the general public. Contact Shieldaig Lodge Hotel (*telephone* 044 583 250).

## KERRY

This is a small, short spate river which has been harnessed by the Hydroelectric Board. Loch Bad an Sgalaig has been dammed, denying salmon access any farther upstream, but the scheme has its positive side as well. Compensation flow and intermittent generation flows protect the Kerry from the worst effects of a summer drought. Even so, it retains its spate river characteristic, and fish are not expected until after the first spate in July. After that, they may continue to be caught after any spate which brings fresh fish in off the tide right through until October. Standard tackle and techniques for West Highland rivers can work very well, with the emphasis being largely on the pursuit of salmon. For some reason, few sea-trout enter or are caught on the Kerry.

A great deal of work has been done, and improvements accomplished, by the Gairloch Angling Association, who lease the fishing from the local estate.

## Season

11 February to 31 October (best July–September).

## Access

Visitors seeking permission to fish the Kerry should contact:

Creag Mor Hotel
Gairloch
Wester Ross
*Telephone* 0445 2068

## EWE AND LOCH MAREE

I have to admit straight away that I am swithering as to what I should say about Loch Maree and the River Ewe which drains it into the sea. You see, this system has long had the reputation of being the heavyweight champion of those systems of long loch and short river systems, which are capable of producing fantastic sport, primarily with sea-trout, and also with salmon. But the champion has taken a few heavy punches. At this moment it is hard to say whether or not it will stage a comeback. The quantity and quality of its catches have dropped alarmingly. The reasons may be complex, but I would be looking first at the intensive netting of sandeels, which are the mainstay of the sea-trout's diet while at sea, and the massive increase in seal predation. Seals have been reported swimming right up the river and even up to the head of the loch in pursuit of Maree's silver migrants.

So, bearing all that in mind, let me describe the Ewe and Loch Maree perhaps as they were, and how we all wish them to be again, when the sea-trout and salmon can find plenty to eat, and not be eaten so often themselves.

## Season

*Ewe*   11 February to 30 September.
*Loch Maree*   11 February to 12 October.

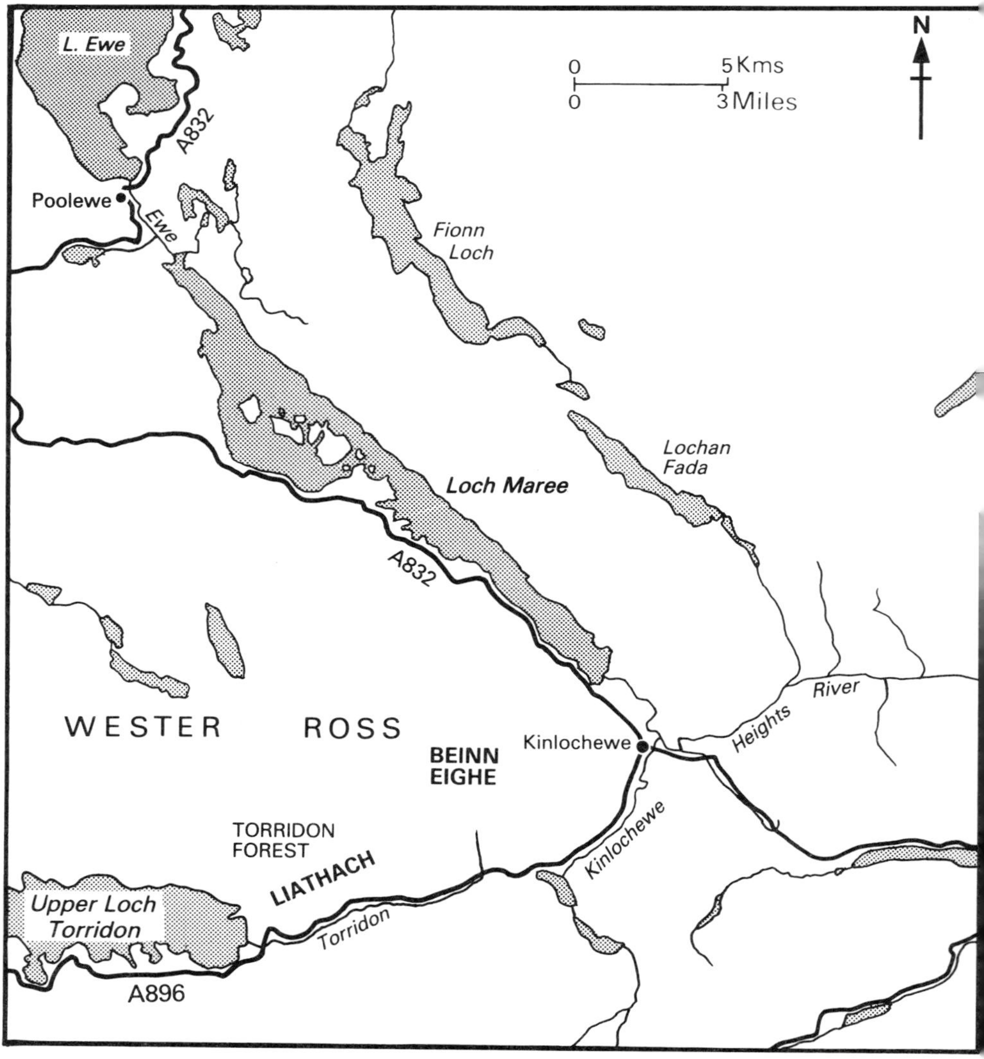

Map 15   *Loch Maree and Rivers Ewe, Kinlochewe and Heights*

## THE RIVER EWE

A short name for a short river. Indeed, the Ewe is recognized as one of the shortest rivers in Scotland, being little more than one mile in length from where it flows out of Loch Maree below the Garden Pool and Top Narrows down to the sea. There are, in fact, three 'Narrows' on this top section of the Ewe: Upper, Middle and

Lower. From the fisherman's point of view, it has to be seen that there is very little fall in the narrows and, therefore, it is only in times of high water, to quicken the pace, that they can show their best. And, as on all sluggish river stretches, a wind to ruffle the water's surface is a great help to the fisherman. Given these conditions of water and wind, Top and Middle Narrows are good salmon pools throughout the season, and Lower Narrows can produce salmon from its tail.

Below Lower Narrows the character of the Ewe is transformed. From here to the sea is a tumbling succession of fine holding pools punctuated with white-water rapids. Fine pools indeed: the Tee Pool, Macordies, Hen, Manse and the Flats. Below the Flats, the river divides around an island, built by man many years ago to aid the netting of the harvest of salmon and sea-trout. There are useful pools on either side of the island whose tails race together into the Sea Pool, which is tidal and can be excellent for fishing, particularly at times of low water.

## LOCH MAREE

Loch Maree is fed by an immense catchment area, much of which drains into the head of the loch through the Kinlochewe River. The other main feeder streams are the Glendocherty Burn and the Heights River. But there are numerous others, all flowing into what has been described as the most ruggedly beautiful loch in Britain – a classic in the style of long, narrow lochs of the West Highland type. The loch is fished from two main areas – the head of the loch is fished by boats out from Kinlochewe and the lower half of the loch by boats out from the Loch Maree Hotel. The loch is studded with islands opposite the hotel, many of which are famous for historic as well as geographical reasons. It is the water around and between them that offers the greatest interest for fishermen in their steadily drifting boats, for here are the great beats of Loch Maree, where heroic battles have been fought with mighty salmon and giant sea-trout fooled by the cleverly fished team of wet flies or the flying dap.

Loch Maree is roughly 14 miles long from Kinlochewe down to the Top Narrows.

### Fish

Salmon may be caught on river pools such as the Top and Middle Narrows on the opening day of the season. However, the best time

*Getting the circulation going on Loch Stack*

of the season is normally in July. This is the time for small flies and a sensitive approach, when the fisherman never really knows whether the next take will be from a salmon, a grilse, a mature sea-trout or a finnock. And the July salmon are all superbly fresh as they do not tarry in the river but head straight up to the loch, unlike a significant proportion of August and September fish. Sea-trout cannot be reasonably expected to run before mid-June.

On the loch the season does not really get under way until April, when boats out from Kinlochewe start to troll round the top end of the loch for early-season salmon. Yes, it is perhaps surprising, but it is the top rather than the middle and bottom of Loch Maree that is best relied upon for early-season salmon sport.

After this opening spree, Maree fishers start to think seriously about sea-trout when the runs start in mid-June. Traditionally, big sea-trout were the vanguards of runs of more numerous but smaller fish. In the 1960s, a great decade for game fishing, Maree more than maintained its reputation for producing sea-trout in double figures and up to 20 lb. Then came UDN (ulcerative dermal necrosis) and these big, multi-return sea-trout were virtually wiped out. Disease passed, and numbers started to return, as well as increasing weights. At the end of the season of 1979 Loch Maree Hotel boats alone took 1,448 sea-trout for a total weight of 4,434 lb, with a very significant proportion of fish between 5 and 10 lb. Ten years later catches are but a fraction of these amounts.

## Dapping

The Ewe produces sport to fairly standard West Highland tackle and techniques. Early-season fishing on the loch is virtually all trolling with Toby spoons, Rapalas, and the like. But once June is in, and thoughts turn to Maree's sea-trout, while some will be taken on traditional loch-style fly fishing the single most popular method on Maree is, without a doubt, the dap. Indeed, it could be said that Maree is the home of dapping for sea-trout, and what it has become internationally famous for.

Dapping stems, perhaps, from an earlier generation's attempts to present a live, struggling insect to sea-trout and trout. Those early fishermen had seen large windborne insects such as the cranefly (also known as the Jenny or daddy-long-legs) as well as moths, flying beetles and so on being blown on to the surface of the loch, and sea-trout rising wildly to take them.

The solution was to pay the local youngsters to catch insects which could be impaled upon the hook or – where small boys ready and willing to earn some pocket money were not numerous or the natural insects themselves were in short supply – to tie up artificial flies to mimic the natural.

Now, such a fly could be presented in the mode of a dry fly, on standard fly rod and line, but these early fishermen were nothing if not inventive, and their solution was to use a long rod and a very light line that would blow out from the rod tip ahead of the drifting boat. You will still see and hear dapping described as 'blow-line fishing' in certain circles and early publications. The fly, natural or artificial, was attached by a short length of gut (in later years, nylon) which was attached to the end of the light line. Floss silk was the normal choice for the line, though synthetics are now the thing, and this would billow out on the wind then, as the rod tip was lowered, the fly would alight on the waves, to be taken or not, such is the way of fishing, by a waiting sea-trout. As simple, and yet as complicated, as that.

Nowadays, while the natural cranefly remains the popular choice in Ireland, virtually all Maree dappers, as on all Scottish sea-trout lochs, have turned to artificials. Some of these are tied as imitations, but such is the inventiveness of the fly dresser that it does not end there. Some dapping flies are quite fantastic creations, with split bucktail wings and tails rather in the manner of a Grey or Red Wulff, while others are beefed-up versions of traditional wet flies that we might choose to fish on the top dropper position of a traditional wet-fly cast.

Take the case of a standard Black Pennell. It might be tied on a size 8 or 10 hook. The throat hackle is black, as is the body under the silver tinsel rib. The tail is a touch of tippet. Now transplant that dressing, but on a size 6 or 4 low-water salmon hook. By the use of a dozen or more stiff cock hackles, the single black hackle is transformed into something looking like a sweep's brush. To increase the buoyancy, the tippet tail might be replaced with a bunch of yellow bucktail. And now you have a useful dapping fly. Or you might have tied it on a 1-inch plastic tube and armed it with a wicked little treble hook, for sea-trout that rise to the dap are notoriously difficult to catch.

Modern dapping rods come in many forms. A carbon salmon fly rod of 15–17 feet proves no mean tool. The most popular alternative, however, is undoubtedly the telescopic fibre-glass dapping rod as made and marketed by Shakespeare tackle. In various lengths up to 17 feet, such a rod has the great advantage of being easy to stow away safely, besides the fact that they are extremely good value. Fill a fly reel spool with braided backing. Attach a rod-length of synthetic dapping floss, knotting it every yard with a simple overhand knot to stop the filaments flying apart. Then loop-to-loop a yard of 12-lb nylon to the floss and attach your dapping fly to the end of this, and you are ready to dap.

I am not alone in finding dapping a fascinating method of taking loch sea-trout. It is also remarkably productive. I, and many others, do not see it as an entirely passive activity. A slight dipping of the rod tip or a swing to the side will cause the big fly to dance and roll, cutting a wake through the wave crests and troughs. Then up comes a sea-trout from deep water with a mighty bang!

Next comes the excitement as well as the frustration of dapping. Whatever fly or hooks we employ and whatever the action we take, it seems inevitable that we will only hook a small proportion of the sea-trout we rise. Fish leap and splash at the fly; they lash and thrash at it. Only sometimes does a big head with open mouth appear to suck in and engulf the dap.

Experience shows that sea-trout are far easier hooked if they come to a bob fly. It also shows that the dap rises significantly more. If only we could bring together the hooking attributes of the bob with the attractive properties of the dap . . . but then, as they say, there is more to fishing than catching fish and, to an even greater extent, there is more to dapping than catching sea-trout.

## Access

The river is owned by the Scatwell Estate and inquiries should be addressed to:

The Scatwell Estate Office
Scatwell
by Muir of Ord
Ross-shire

Loch Maree Hotel and its fishings are tied up in a timeshare scheme. Weeks are occasionally available, however. For details contact:

Loch Maree Hotel
by Poolewe
Ross and Cromarty
*Telephone* 044 589 200

Kinlochewe Chalets have boats on the loch. Contact:

Peter MacDonald
*Telephone* 044 584 253

Kinlochewe Hotel at Kinlochewe also has a boat for the loch and may be able to offer the services of a gillie. *Telephone* 044 584 253.

Kinlochewe Hotel should also be contacted in regard to fishing the Kinlochewe River, where it has beats on the lower half. This river fishes particularly well on the heels of a spate to draw fish up from Loch Maree. Given a wet summer, as in 1988, the river fishes extremely well. Indeed, the record season of 1988 produced 87 salmon and 267 sea-trout.

## GRUINARD AND BROOM

It is not my intention in writing this book to give details of those rivers that are fished privately. Therefore there seems little point in saying very much about the Gruinard or Little Gruinard except, perhaps, to mention that the Gruinard, despite some measure of decline in recent seasons, has long enjoyed the reputation of providing some of the finest sea-trout sport available, and a place where they will readily take a dry fly. But the fishing is all in private hands.

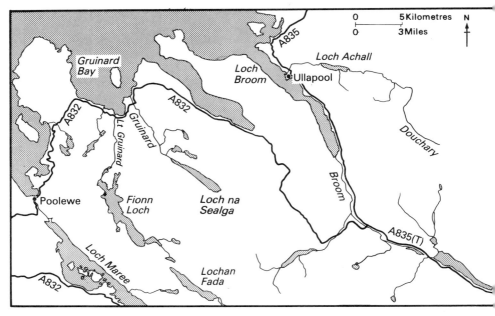

Map 16    *Rivers Gruinard and Broom*

Much the same could be said of the Broom, except that the Inverbroom Estate which owns all but a small section of the left bank does occasionally let beats, the best time here being July and August.

In the modern age, the Broom, which flows into the head of salt-water Loch Broom, has been harnessed for power generation and, with its headwaters diverted, is reliant upon compensation flow. It is, nevertheless, very much a spate river and subject to the normal needs of rain and spate to bring up salmon and grilse in July. Sea-trout fishing is still good, though, as on virtually all these western waters, not as good as it has been. Fishing on the Broom is by fly only.

**Season**

11 February to 31 October (best June–July).

**Access**

As stated, the Gruinard rivers are entirely in private ownership and use, but there may occasionally be opportunity to fish the Inverbroom Estate Water. Contact:

Sharpe & Matheson
Inverbroom
Ross and Cromarty

## ULLAPOOL

High on the hills of Inverlael Forest is the source of the River
Douchary. Farther downstream its name changes to the Rhiddor-
roch, which flows into Loch Achall. The outflow from Loch Achall
is the Ullapool river, which flows into saltwater Loch Broom just
north of the popular tourist town of Ullapool. Little wonder that
it is popular – a busy fishing harbour and ferry port set on
a bewitching coastline, with the magical hills and mountains for a
perfect backdrop. But while some holidaymakers will pray for
sunshine and clear blue skies, others will be perversely tapping at
barometers and hoping for rain. For the rain brings spates, and
these are just what is required to bring fish into the river and up to
the loch.

There are 3 beats on the Ullapool river. The middle beat is
generally regarded as the best. The loch is noted for sea-trout, with
good trout fishing as well, but only an occasional salmon is taken.

### Season

11 February to 31 October (best July–August).

### Access

Permission to fish the beats or loch should be sought by making
inquiries to any of the following:

Highland Coastal Estates
Ullapool
Ross and Cromarty

Lochbroom Hardware
Shore Street
Ullapool
Ross and Cromarty

Anchor Centre
Argyle Street
Ullapool
*Telephone* 0854 2488

## GARVIE AND LOCH OSCAIG

This little system is different – very different. The rivers Garvie and Oscaig are, in fact, little more than the feeder streams between a series of lochs, and it is the small lochs that provide the bulk of the sport. Indeed, one man who has fished in the Garvie and Oscaig told me that he considered the Garvie, which flows into the sea from Loch Garvie, just too steep for fishing – the salmon and sea-trout must be forced to climb it as if they were going up near-vertical stairs.

Loch Garvie itself is a small and reedy loch, but Loch Oscaig is that little bit larger and, it is said, can normally be the better bet for grilse and sea-trout during the peak months of July and August.

### Season

11 February to 31 October (summer best).

### Access

Permits to fish the Garvie and Loch Oscaig are to be had from the Summer Isles Hotel at Achiltibuie (*telephone* 085 482 282).

## POLLY

The Polly is a small but interesting river which forms the outflow to two lochs. These are Loch Sionascaig and Loch Doire na h-Airbe.

For some distance below the lochs, the river flows swiftly but, in its lower reaches, the gradient falls away and it becomes somewhat sluggish.

Incidentally, on the tributary that flows out of Loch Sionascaig there are a number of other, smaller lochs.

### Season

11 February to 31 October (best June–August).

### Fishing

A significant number of the fish entering the Polly during the peak months of June through to August have a habit of resting in the slower stretches of the lower river. The salmon fisherman who knows what he is about will be quick to fish such stretches when a wind ruffles the surface. The traditional method then, in order to swim the fly or flies attractively, is backing up – casting fairly square and taking a couple of steps upstream and handlining before making the next cast. In this way you fish the pool from bottom to top. However, those who prefer the more conventional approach of fishing from top to bottom may swim the flies entirely by handlining and fishing down in the normal way. And if you feel certain that there are taking fish in a pool you might even fish from top to bottom by handlining, then immediately fish it back to the top by backing up. For summer work, a duet of flies can work well – perhaps a size 10 Stoat on the point and a Shrimp Fly on the dropper.

## Access

It is possible to gain permission to fish either the lochs or the river. The Royal Hotel in Ullapool, some 20 miles away, has fishing for their guests on the river. *Telephone* 0854 2181. Permission can also be had from Mrs A. MacLeod (*telephone* 05714 252). For the lochs also, approach Inverpolly Estate Office (*telephone* 05714 252).

## KIRKAIG

Although the catchment area of the Kirkaig covers roughly 80 square miles, a considerable amount compared to a typical West Highland river, with an extensive system of lochs on its headwaters it is only the first 2 miles up from the tide that are of interest to the salmon fisherman. On inspecting the river the reason is obvious, for it is just 2 miles from the estuary to the sheer face of the 50-foot-high Falls of Kirkaig. Migratory fish simply cannot pass any farther upstream.

In effect, then, the salmon and sea-trout's environment is severely restricted. It must be sufficient, however, to provide adequate breeding and nursery areas for both salmon and sea-trout for, as the fishing records show, the catches are significant for the area both in terms of quality and quantity.

But it is not simply the fish that give the Kirkaig such great appeal for many fishermen, however fine those salmon may be. The Kirkaig also offers its own sporting challenge, simply in terms of being able to fish it effectively. For here is a raging torrent down a rocky gorge where boulders and rocks the size of a crofter's cottage may split the stream. The succession of rocky faces and high, heather-clad banks makes this a river where climbing boots rather than waders are the thing, certainly when you are fishing the upper beat, next to the Falls.

There are, in fact, three beats on the river. These are the Upper, Middle and Lower. The coastal road from Lochinver passes along and over the Lower beat and so this offers the easiest access. There are 7 pools on this beat, starting with the Heather Pool at the top, which is generally reckoned to be the best on this stretch, and going right down to the Sea Pool, which seldom yields salmon but can be very good for sea-trout.

There are 10 pools on the Middle beat. Those that regulars would mark out for particular attention are the Upper Red Pool, Little Kirkaig and the Hazel.

The Upper beat is, to my eyes, the most attractive and challenging. It starts at the Kirkaig Falls Pool and ends with the MacKenzie Stream to give a total of 13 pools, and includes the Little Falls Pool, which is reckoned by many to be the best on the river.

## Season

11 February to 15 October (best July–September).

## Fish and Fishing

The period from April to June may see an odd fish being caught from the Kirkaig, but sport becomes that little bit more predictable from the end of June onwards. After that it is just a case of waiting for rain to raise the river into spate and bring in fish. Sport then continues through to September. Indeed, the month of September can be particularly good if the heavy runs of salmon and grilse have been held back from entering the river by summer drought.

Kirkaig has something of a reputation for producing a good size of salmon, particularly when compared with other West Highland rivers. The average weight may be as high as 10 lb, and fish up to 40 lb have been known in the past.

## Tackle and Technique

The tackle and techniques for fishing the Kirkaig deserve mention in their own right. Heavy salmon in high water in a rocky, boulder-strewn stream tend to write their own rule books, and the angler simply must be prepared for them. And note that the Kirkaig rule is fly only.

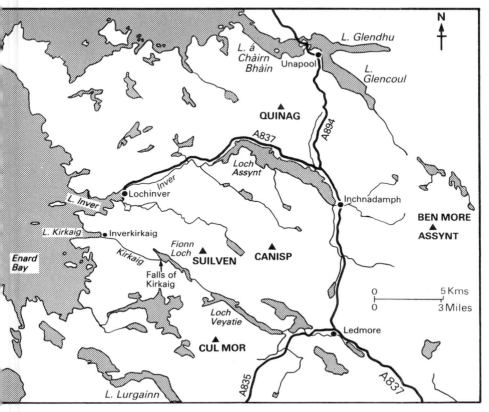

Map 17    *Rivers Kirkaig and Inver*

First, a word about flies. The Kirkaig has retained a reputation as being one river where the traditional classic patterns of fly are still to be found in general use. Look at the fishing register in the local hotel and you will see salmon taken on the Yellow Torrish, the Silver Doctor, the Black Doctor, the Thunder and Lightning, and so on. Many might say that this is nothing but a local fashion. I know that many years ago, when I visited the Kirkaig, I was frankly amazed to see such flies tied on single hooks up to 7/0 in size. Tubes and Waddingtons were certainly used as well, but why had they not been adopted almost exclusively, as on most Scottish salmon rivers?

Leaving aside the relative attractions of the various designs, to the eyes of both fish and fisherman, I do believe that to understand the retention of the single hook on such a water you have to picture the scene when a heavy fish is hooked in a deep and powerful cauldron pool, when the salmon decides that he is going to return to the sea. True, the big single hook may not be the best thing for initial hooking but, once it has got a hold, it does tend to stay put. The thinner wire of a smaller treble hook, fished in conjunction with a tube or Waddington, is more likely to either open out or cut through the flesh of the fish's mouth, and thus be torn away.

This very real possibility of the fight degenerating into a tug of war as a salmon heads downstream and the fisherman cannot follow also means that the Kirkaig is no place for light leaders. In high water, there is every reason to regard 15 lb as an absolute minimum, and many would prefer to give themselves an even greater margin for safety. It is not simply a matter of a straight pull on a fish. There is also the very real chance that the leader will be drawn over the rocks and boulders that make up the river bed in many places.

Equally, it is not a wise move, certainly when big flies are being used in high water, to fish with a rod that lacks backbone. In the modern age of carbon fibre rods there is everything to be said for a powerful 15-footer.

Naturally, all that I have said applies only to times when the water is falling after a spate, and the chances of contacting salmon are at their peak. As the water falls to summer levels, however, there is no alternative but to fish that little bit finer and with more delicacy. Now patterns such as the Hairy Mary, the Stoat's Tail, the Munro Killer, the Shrimp Fly and so on, fished in sizes 8 and 10, come into their own. If you wish, now that the current has slackened somewhat, the length and power of the rod might also be reduced, but remember the advantages of a long rod for roll and Spey casting – very useful skills for those who would fish the Kirkaig.

Finally, I should mention one minor tactic that can be employed to great effect on the Kirkaig, as it can on many Highland rivers with swift, rocky flows. It is dibbling. I describe this technique in greater detail under the Helmsdale (page 150), but the basics are to fish with a dropper some 4 feet above the point fly, and to make the dropper riffle across the water surface by raising the rod tip and, if necessary, recovering line at the same time. This method can be particularly effective when used in the fast stream at the head of a pool. Various patterns and sizes of flies can be used but many choose to follow the local example of fishing a 1/0 and a 3/0 traditional flies together when the water is falling after a spate. Also, in fairly recent times, the long-winged Elver fly, tied to Arthur Ransome's pattern, has become very popular for use with the dibbling technique.

*The solid resistance of a Loch More (Sutherland) sea-trout*

## Access

Fishing on the Kirkaig is available to guests of the Inver Lodge Hotel which, like the river, is owned by Assynt Estate. Contact:

Inver Lodge Hotel
Lochinver
Sutherland
*Telephone* 057 14 496

Alternatively, and for information on the Kirkaig and neighbouring River Inver, contact:

The Factor
Assynt Estate Office
Lochinver
Sutherland
*Telephone* 057 14 203

## INVER AND LOCH ASSYNT

The waters tumbling from the steep mountains of Inchnadamph and Ben More Assynt join and flow through lochs before eventually emerging as the River Loanan, which feeds into the 5-mile-long and dramatically beautiful Loch Assynt. The river that flows out of the loch on a 6-mile journey through a glen which for much of its length is richly wooded is known as the Inver. A rich, tumbling river cascading past ancient silver birch and modern conifer plantations, and a river that can, in a good season, produce as many as 400 salmon to the lucky rods.

### Season

11 February to 31 October (best June–August).

### Fish and Fishing

A catch of 400 salmon in a good season. Some of these fish will be taken during the early months but their numbers are insignificant when compared with the heavy runs that occur normally in the summer months of June, July and August, though a dry summer can mean that September may become a prime month. So it is during the summer that Inver rods prepare for sport with salmon, grilse and sea-trout, a good proportion of which will run up into Loch Assynt. The loch is fished by five boats owned by the Inchnadamph Hotel, who might expect their guests, in a good season, to take 50 or 60 salmon and a number of sea-trout.

As a word of caution, however – and I am talking now about those catch figures for the River Inver – it must be remembered that the river is most productive in its lower half, which is very nearly entirely private.

### Tackle and Techniques

Standard loch tactics will work well on Loch Assynt – although, as is always the case, there will usually be somebody in the hotel bar who is prepared to tell you of this or that deadly pattern or minor technique which will, in his estimation, work the charm!

As for the river, standard river tactics tend to be the thing, with many regulars being prepared to try the added attractions of a dropper. If nothing else, this allows the fisherman to present two patterns of different size to salmon at one and the same time – say, a

Shrimp Fly on the point and a Hairy Mary on the dropper, in sizes 10 and 8 when the water is not too high.

Those preparing to fish some of the stronger pools in high water might care to read the comments that have been written in regard to the Kirkaig.

## Access

*Loch Assynt*

> Willie Morrison
> The Inchnadamph Hotel
> Inchnadamp
> Assynt
> Lochinver
> Sutherland
> *Telephone* 05712 202

*River Inver*

> Inver Lodge Hotel
> Lochinver
> Sutherland
> *Telephone* 057 14 496

## LOCHS STACK AND MORE

Lochs Stack and More are two large and significant waters on the headwaters of the Laxford river. The river is not discussed here because it is fished privately, but it is widely recognised as one of the most productive rivers in northern Scotland. This is, of course, why the two lochs have built up such a high reputation, particularly Loch Stack, which is far-famed for the quality of its sea-trout catches. Forty years ago it was regarded as the best in Scotland.

The course of the system is from the top of Kinlochbrae and into Loch More. This is connected to Loch Stack by what is little more than a channel and lochan.

The rather odd shape of Loch Stack – something like a capital H with a long arm – can be a little bit disorientating to first-time visitors. Whatever the description, it is what lies under the surface of a loch fishery that is most important, and Loch Stack is blessed with a great variety of rocks, banks and bays which create a near-ideal loch environment for sea-trout and salmon.

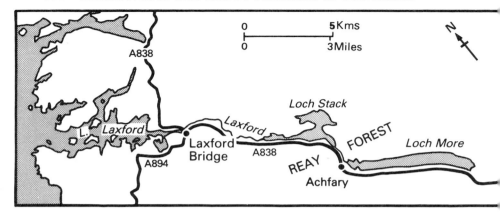

Map 18    *Lochs Stack and More*

## Season

11 February to 31 October (best June–August).

## Fish and Fishing

The peak runs of sea-trout, grilse and salmon up the Laxford and into Lochs Stack and More are expected in the period from June to August. Things being what they are in the modern age, catches are not what they were in the past, but the lochs can still show excellent sport on their day.

In comparing Loch Stack with Loch More, one interesting fact emeges beyond simply noting that the former is more productive than the latter. It is that while Loch Stack is well suited to fairly conventional sea-trout tactics with a team of wet flies, Loch More tends to do better for the dap. This has, I think, a lot to do with depth of water. Loch Stack is, overall, rather shallower than Loch More. Certainly Stack has its deeper parts but, as I say, generally you are fishing over rather shallower water. Dapping has the reputation, by presenting a rather larger fly, of drawing fish up through a considerable depth of water. This is something that might profitably be applied to a large number of sea-trout lochs. Experienced loch fishermen will be able to list various drifts that seem to produce their best to the wet-fly fisherman, and others where the dap can really score. In making a choice between dap and wet fly, it seems that depth of water may well be at least one of the factors to be considered.

**Access**

Information on day permits to fish the lochs is available from:

Westminster Estate Office
Achfary
by Lairg
Sutherland
*Telephone* 097 184 221

Scourie Hotel, Scourie (*telephone* 0971 2393) can also arrange fishing on these lochs, as well as on more than 300 hill lochs for trout.

# 6  The Western Isles

Called the Outer Hebrides by geographers but by few Scots, the
Western Isles are a string of islands nestling in the Atlantic. Starting
from the north they are Lewis, Harris, North Uist, Benbecula,
South Uist and Barra. And for generations of sportsmen they have
been regarded as a fishing paradise.

This book is concerned only with salmon and sea-trout fisheries,
but I feel I can scarcely ignore the fact that somebody who took the
time to count discovered that there were more than 200 trout lochs
on the islands, with free-rising, wild-fighting brownies to snatch at
the fisherman's team of flies. Naturally enough, the salmon and
sea-trout fisheries are not so numerous but, even so, they offer a
great kaleidoscope of sport, on both lochs and small rivers.

As to the tackle and technique that will suit most conditions to be
encountered on the Western Isles, personal tastes obviously differ.
Some folk may care to carry a double-handed salmon rod, 13 or 14
feet of carbon fibre, but others find more fun is to be had in sticking
with a single-handed rod for their salmon and grilse as well as their
sea-trout. Of course, if the single-hander is to be the sort of
all-rounder that will cope with both river and loch, it should not be
too short. Some will settle on a 10-footer, though others, myself
included, would choose something a little longer.

What flies to take? Again, the traditional favourites are found to
do well in Hebridean waters. Perhaps the Stoat's Tail would come
top of the list among the widely popular black patterns for salmon
and grilse. For sea-trout you could do worse than to stick with flies
such as the Peter Ross, the Silver Invicta, the Mallard and Claret,
the Cinnamon and Gold, and, for the bob position, a faily bushy
palmered fly such as one of the Zulus, or perhaps a Dark Mackerel
or a Wickham's Fancy. Black Pennells are normally associated with
the bob position also but, if tied with a long, mobile, thin throat
hackle, they can be quite deadly when fished on the point of a
sea-trout cast. And I would not travel to Hebridean waters without
a Goat's Toe and a Camasunary Killer.

## Season and Best Times

Virtually all the Hebridean fisheries have a season for salmon and
sea-trout extending from February into October. However, little

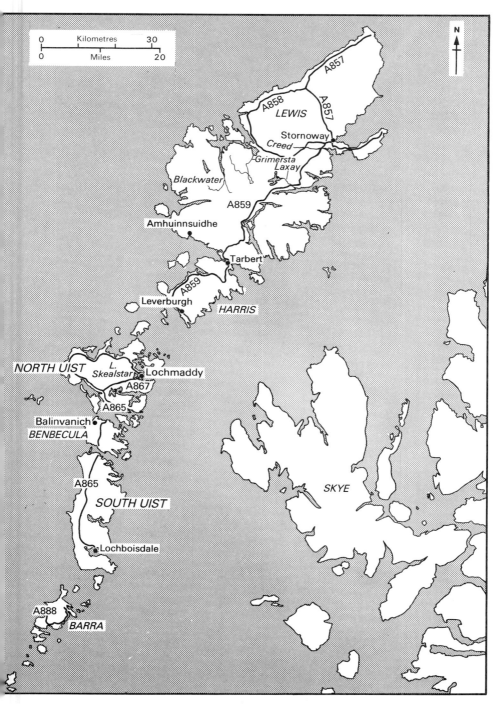

Map 19　*The Western Isles*

activity will be expected until June, after which it may continue through to the end of the season.

## LEWIS

Despite the fact that a great deal of the salmon and sea-trout fishing on Lewis is private and strictly preserved, there are a number of opportunities for those in search of first-class sport with migratory species.

## RIVER CREED OR GRETA

If you telephoned me to say that you were on your way to Lewis but had forgotten to arrange any fishing before you set off, my advice would be to make inquiries as to the availability of a rod on the River Creed. This is not because it is the best but, rather, because it is the one most likely to be available to the casual visitor, and because it is let on a daily basis at reasonable cost. Fishing on the river is fly-only.

There are 5 miles of river to be fished and two lochs. For an extra charge, a boat is available on one of these, namely Loch a' Chlachain.

Sea-trout can be expected in the river and loch as early as June but the main run of salmon comes that little bit later, in July in a normal season.

The river is divided into 3 single-rod beats, which rotate on a daily basis. Thus a fisherman who fishes the full six-day fishing week will have two days on each beat. The loch is fished by two boats, each with one rod fishing. Indeed, this is typical of Hebridean loch fisheries, which, because of their size and the possible disturbance factor, are best fished across rather than down the wind on the drift. If you choose to fish across the wind, of course, perhaps searching out a leeward shore, then there must be somebody with you to man the oars.

## Access

Inquiries for access to the river and loch should be directed to the Estate Office, Stornoway Trust (*telephone* 0851 2002).

# BLACKWATER

There is little doubting that the Grimersta is the jewel in the crown of Hebridean fisheries, but it would be a hard thing to state with certainty whether it is the Creed, the Laxay or the Blackwater that runs in to second place. It is certainly a gem, this Blackwater, if not perhaps a jewel. The best of the holding pools and fishing are in the lower part of the river. In the rather peaty water, a fly with a touch of yellow or orange, such as a Garry, can work very well.

## Access

Full details of what fishing may be had on the Blackwater are available from the Garynahine Estate Office (*telephone* 085172 209).

# FHORSA

Situated close to Uig on the west coast of Lewis, the River Fhorsa can yield excellent sport on its day. The fishing, which is for up to six rods, is let together with lodge accommodation.

## Access

A detailed brochure of the Fhorsa fishing is available from:

Finlayson Hughes
Estates Office
Bonar Bridge
Sutherland
*Telephone* 08632 553

Fishing in this area, although not on this particular river, is available from other sources. Fishing mainly on lochs with boat and gillie may be had from Scaliscro Lodge (*telephone* 085175 325).

# GRIMERSTA

The Grimersta is a truly great fishery in a national as well as a Hebridean context. To describe it in as basic terms as possible, it is a short river of less than 2 miles, above which is a chain of five main lochs. The highest of these lochs is Loch Langavat, which, at 7 miles long, is the longest loch in the Hebrides. In addition to the five main lochs on the system, there are numerous side lochs, but

*This 23 lb springer fell to a small hairwing treble on a floating line*

only a couple of these can be considered as significant from the fishing point of view. It all adds up to make a highly prolific fishery system. Indeed, it is said that size for size it is second to none.

Virtually the entire fishery system is under the control of Grimersta Estate Ltd, which is controlled by a syndicate. The river and lochs are run as a model of fishery management and, it is worth noting, create employment for 25 people in what is otherwise a remote and sparsely populated area. The river, lochs, lodge and boats are all carefully maintained. Fly only is the general rule but trolling with fly is allowed on one loch and on Loch Langavat, where the ownership is shared between seven estates, trolling with fly or spinner is not only allowed but also the principal method.

Members of the Grimersta syndicate and their personal guests rely heavily, when fishing the lochs with fly, on fishing a 'little and large' combination. By that I mean that on a long but light rod they will fish a tiny double or wisp of a tube fly on the point of the leader, but something much larger – say a size 4 or 6 – on the dropper. Salmon will take this dropper, but its principal role is to act as a piscatorial dinner gong, catching the attention of a fish which may sheer away from the oversized dropper only to take solidly on the tiny point fly. Of course, fishermen have their own individual views and one member of the syndicate told me that he fishes more normal, smaller flies on the bob, and takes his share of fish, except that he feels it significant that he, unlike others, takes a good proportion on the dropper. Whatever . . . if you choose to fish the Grimersta in the traditional manner, good patterns to try in the dropper position include the Elver Fly and the Muddler Minnow, with its head of clipped deer hair, to create maximum wake.

## Access

What chance do you have of getting to fish the Grimersta? Until recent times, unless you were lucky enough to be a syndicate member or close friend, the chances were virtually nil. And the same is still true today if you are talking about fishing the Grimersta after the main runs of fish are expected in June. However, there is a small run of early-season fish which can put in an appearance before the syndicate fishing gets into swing, and it may be possible to accommodate small parties of fishing guests. The man to contact with your inquiries is the Fishery Manager (*telephone* 085172 358).

## LAXAY

If anybody has taken the trouble of establishing exactly which of a maze of streams and lochans that dot the headwaters of this river is its recognizable source, then I have yet to hear of it. Many of them do, however, drain into Loch Trealval and the river flows out of this loch for a distance of 3 miles before flowing into Loch Valtos. After Valtos, it is just a short run of less than 1 mile to the salt water of Loch Erisort.

The river fishing is largely confined to the lower section, which is fished by one or two rods. There are three main pools. These are simply, if not romantically, named Top, Middle and Lower. This is where the majority of fish are taken, either by the owners or their tenants, but there is also fishing on the river above Loch Valtos.

The loch is divided into beats, each with a boat and gillie. Incidentally, I personally would always choose to fish one rod in a boat when fishing for migratory fish in Hebridean lochs, and employ the across rather than downwind fishing technique.

History shows that there has in the past been an early-season run of salmon into the Laxay. In modern times, however, the season is not expected to get really under way before July, with the fishing continuing through to October.

## Access

The Laxay and Loch Valtos are on the 38,000 acre Soval Estate, which can also offer trout fishing on more than 200 lochs. There is a lodge which provides full board, with lets being weekly or fortnightly and for a minimum of five rods. For full details contact:

Richard Kershaw
Joseph Holt Plc
Derby Brewery
Cheetham
Manchester
*Telephone* 061 834 3285

## ISLE OF HARRIS

Harris is the southerly half of the same principal island as Lewis, and it is at Tarbert that the ferry from mainland Scotland arrives. For some folk, the name of Harris is most closely associated with the world-famous tweeds, but for me the thoughts are rather different. I wrote in an earlier book of a time when I caught my first Hebridean fish while drifting a Harris loch: 'I was not yet in my teens, and many seasons have passed since then, but that hard-fighting and wild spirit still haunts my mind. It flashes back through crystal clear waters, jigging and reeling to rid itself of the tiny Wickham's Fancy embedded in its jaw.' We were staying at the Harris Hotel in Tarbert, and fishing the Laxadale Lochs.

As on Lewis, many of the Harris fisheries are maintained as private affairs, but that is not to say that there are not plenty of opportunities for the visitor.

## SCARISTA

Borve Lodge Estates have loch fishing for salmon and sea-trout at Scarista. Unfortunately, for those who like to plan ahead, fishing cannot be taken in advance as the fishing is let on an occasional, daily, basis. Fishing at its best from July through to the end of October. Apply to:

Tony Schorr
The Factor
Borve Lodge Estates
Isle of Harris
*Telephone* 08598 5202

## HORSACLEIT

Fishings are let in conjunction with Horsacleit Lodge on a weekly and fortnightly basis. This is fly-only fishing and perhaps it should be mentioned that the main appeal is the excellent brown-trout fishing on Loch Drinishader and other lochs. Then, when a spate brings the Horsacleit into spate and sets sea-trout and the occasional salmon in a running and, with luck, a taking mood, the concentration shifts to the river. No bad thing really. Personally, I would always ensure that I had the back-up of good trout fishing when planning a trip to the spate streams of the West and the Hebrides, where the chances of sport with migratory species are so heavily dependent upon rainfall.

### Access

Bookings should be made to:

Mr C. J. Lucas
Warnham Park
Horsham
Sussex
*Telephone* 0403 52295

Occasional day tickets may also be available. Inquiries to the manager, Neil Macdonald (*telephone* 0859 2464).

## LEVERBURGH

Down at Leverburgh, the Rodel Hotel has salmon and sea-trout as well as brown-trout fishing on lochs. Boats are available and gillies can be arranged. The best months are reckoned to be July, August and September, with August being the best for salmon. Contact:

Rodel Hotel
Leverburgh
Isle of Harris
*Telephone* 08598 2210

## NORTH UIST

Virtually all the fishing on North Uist is owned by the North Uist Estates Ltd, Lochmaddy, North Uist, to whom inquiries can be made. However, these fishings can be fished by guests staying at the Lochmaddy Hotel, who can make arrangements for gillies. Boats are available. Besides about 150 lochs – only some of which contain salmon and sea-trout, of course – there are sea pools to be fished. These sea pools, besides producing sea-trout as you would expect, have also been known to produce salmon.

Other than on the sea pools, the fishing is by fly only.

It would be impossible to discuss the North Uist fishings without making mention of the runs into the Skealstar system. While virtually all Hebridean and western waters have to wait until at least June to show any worthwhile level of sport, Skealstar with its chain of lochs has a tradition for being able to show early sport as well, with as many as 40 salmon being taken by the end of May. In the modern era, however, when spring runs are in such delicate balance on all rivers, things are not quite what they once were and, while salmon will certainly be seen in the sea pools as early as April, it is in the months of July, August and September that salmon and sport are more dependable.

Contact Lochmaddy Hotel at Lochmaddy (*telephone* 08763 331).


## SOUTH UIST

Salmon and sea-trout fishing can be had on a number of lochs owned by South Uist Estate, and, as on North Uist, there is fishing to be had in certain sea pools. Grogarry Lodge may be booked with the fishing. For details contact the South Uist Estate Office (*telephone* 08784 301).

Most anglers, however, will choose to fish the South Uist Estate's waters from the Lochboisdale Hotel (*telephone* 08784 332), which can offer ten beats on seven lochs with boats. Given water to bring salmon and sea-trout up from the salt, the fishing will be best from late June until the close of the season at the end of September.

# 7 The North Coast

It would be hard to pick out one particular area of Scotland that could be said to offer the salmon and sea-trout fisherman everything that he desires. The West Coast is a rugged land of wild spate rivers and lochs, in contrast to the great and majestic rivers of the east. Perhaps the solution is to fall between these two extremes. Who knows, but there are certainly many anglers who will champion the cause of the North Coast, stretching across the counties of Sutherland and Caithness, as coming close to the salmon and sea-trout fisherman's idea of heaven.

Of course, find a heaven on earth and, such is the way of things, somebody may have got there before you. Access to rivers such as the Dionard, the Hope and the Naver is very strictly preserved, and

*Using the tailer to land a salmon – some prefer this method to the net*

there is no point in anybody thinking he can simply wave his cheque book and walk straight onto such waters. But that much is true of so many of the best class of salmon and sea-trout rivers in the modern age, when demand exceeds supply, and a man recognizes more than cash value in what he holds in terms of ownership and access.

## DIONARD

The Dionard drains the eastern slopes of Meall Horn, running north to the sea near Cape Wrath, into the Kyle of Durness. There is one loch on the river's course, Loch Dionard, which acts as a filter as well as a reserve of water to steady the spate nature of the river.

The loch itself has enjoyed a fine reputation as a producer of sea-trout. When one considers the problems traditionally involved in gaining access to the loch, it certainly must have been good in order to tempt fishermen to it. Ownership of the loch is divided between three estates, the Gaulin Estate, the Reay Forest Estate and Gobernuisgach. The approach from the latter two used to involve a trek of about 4 hours over rough hill country, accompanied by garron ponies carrying supplies, and the standard plan was to stay overnight in a bothy. I have not been able to ascertain whether these two estates have stuck with this traditional method of treeking in, but the Snowcat and Argocat have become such a part of the remoter Highland scene that I cannot but doubt it.

The upper part of the river is private but on those lower parts to which the fishing public may hope to gain access there are some very good pools for both salmon and sea-trout.

### Season

11 January to 1 October (best June–August).

### Fish and Fishing

While the Dionard yields good numbers of salmon and grilse, it is perhaps best to regard it principally as a sea-trout river. Nevertheless, during the summer months all three fish can be expected to provide some excellent sport. It is a spate river, and rains are required to raise water levels in order for the Dionard to show its best.

With regard to salmon, except during the falling off of a spate when fairly large flies can be used to good effect, it is generally sensible to introduce some sensitivity into your presentation. On any clear-water salmon river, a fine-and-far-off approach can reap its rewards. Little wisps of flies tied on Esmond-Drury-type trebles in patterns such as the Silver Stoat may be tried, perhaps on a single-handed rod that will double for sea-trout. Where the emphasis is more towards casting accuracy than sheer range, more and more fishermen are finding their summer salmon and grilse fun without resorting to a double-hander, though the added benefits of the longer reach and control should not be dismissed too lightly.

When choosing sea-trout flies for the Dionard or any other river, many sea-trout fishermen tend towards the rather cavalier approach of thinking which says that if they are taking then they will take virtually anything. Well, perhaps that is so, but when the sea-trout have been in the river for a while they might need quite a small fly to tempt them, perhaps something like a wee double – say a Peter Ross or a Teal, Blue and Silver tied on a 12 hook.

One of the features of sea-trout fishing is that the farther south you travel the less likely sea-trout are to take in daylight. Applying the reverse, in travelling north you can't get much farther than the Dionard and the Kyle of Durness.

## Access

The upper river, owned by the Gualin Estate, is private. However, it is possible to get fishing on the lower river. Contact:

> Cape Wrath Hotel
> Durness
> Sutherland
> *Telephone* 097181 274

## LOCH HOPE

The Hope system has a very extensive catchment area. Three headwater tributaries join together to form the River Strathmore, which flows into the 6-mile-long Loch Hope. The River Hope flows out of the bottom of Loch Hope on a short journey of barely more than a mile on its way to the salt water of Loch Eriboll. The reason why no more mention is made of the river is that the fishing, while undoubtedly excellent, is kept private.

## Season

12 January to 30 October.

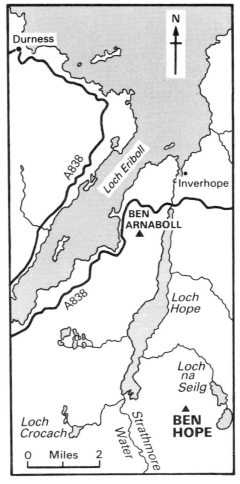

Map 20   *Loch Hope*

## Fish and Fishing

Loch Hope has long enjoyed the reputation of being among Scotland's leading sea-trout lochs. This status may have been called into question by fishermen visiting the loch during the dry season of 1989, but it is hoped that this will prove to be no more than a temporary setback.

The fishing on Loch Hope is by fly only. This rule does, however, allow the use of the dap. Incidentally, the dap has the reputation of being able to rise the larger class of sea-trout from deep-water lies, but there are times when the sea-trout comes up, shows at the fly, but fails to take securely. If your partner is fishing wet fly and he casts quickly to cover the fish, he can often persuade it to take one of his smaller offerings.

Such examples of combined operations with fly and dap hold much food for thought. Is it not possible that by fishing a big fly on the top dropper – say, a heavily hackled Zulu or Palmer on a 6 hook, or a 4 in a big, rolling wave – we can combine the attractions of dap and wet fly at one and the same time? A long loch rod, perhaps a 12-foot single-hander, allows us to fish the bob fly scuttering on the surface for long distances and, even if the fish it rises do not take it, they are now in a position to note the attractions of the fly on the point or middle of the cast.

### Access

Altnaharra Hotel has access to a great deal of fishing (also Loch Naver, below), including Loch Hope, on which they have a number of boats. Contact:

Altnaharra Hotel
by Lairg
Sutherland
*Telephone* 054 981 222

## LOCH NAVER AND RIVERS MALLART AND MUDALE

Loch Meadie is drained by the River Mudale into the 6-mile-long Loch Naver. The River Naver flows out of Loch Naver then continues on its 18-mile journey to the sea, which it enters close to Bettyhill. Just downstream of Loch Naver, the river is joined by a tributary, and this is the Mallart.

The River Naver displays two characteristics. At first it flows across open moorland and then it drops in a fine series of pools through delicious woodlands – enough to steal the heart of any salmon fisherman. And the Naver has more going for it than just good looks. Its reputation in northern Scotland as a producer of salmon and grilse is such that it closely rivals, if perhaps not quite equalling, the Helmsdale. But, unless you are a very lucky person indeed, this will be of little interest, for the fact of the matter is that the river is kept as the privatest of private affairs. On Loch Naver, on the other hand, access is far easier to achieve, as it is on the rivers Mudale and Mallart.

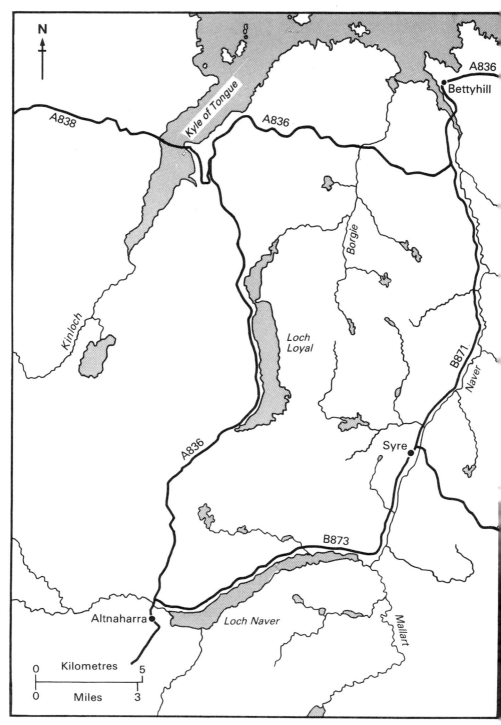

Map 21   *Naver and District*

## Season

12 January to 30 September (best March–April).

## Fish and Fishing

The Naver can produce an odd salmon in January and then numbers build up to create peak spring numbers in April, by when the loch fishing can be excellent. At this early stage of the season trolling is allowed and is normally the most popular method, with Toby spoons, Rapalas and the like. There are three beats and three boats on the loch, which are fished through the Altnaharra Hotel. Later in the season one of these beats is kept for fly fishing only. Altnaharra Hotel also owns the River Mudale, above Loch Naver, which can be relied upon to produce a few salmon in a season. It takes rods on the Mallart tributary up to the start of July as well as taking various weeks on the Borgie and Halladale (see below).

## Access

Naturally, guests of the Altnaharra Hotel are given first choice of the fishing, but if there is any remaining, it may be possible for others to gain permission. Contact:

Altnaharra Hotel
by Lairg
Sutherland
*Telephone* 054 981 222

## HALLADALE

The headwaters of the Halladale, up beyond Forsinard, are close to the headwaters of the Helmsdale. The rivers, however, are very different. The fine Helmsdale pools contrast sharply with the slow, straight nature of the Halladale. The only place that one could describe the Halladale as a 'tumbling stream' is in the Forsinard area but, for the rest of its 20 miles to the sea at Melvich, it appears sluggish and uninspiring. But, my goodness, how looks can deceive!

## Season

12 January to 30 September (best June–September).

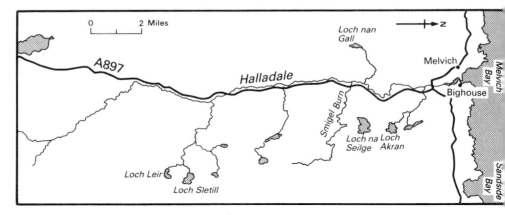

Map 22    *The Halladale*

## Fish and Fishing

The Halladale is very much the spate river, in fish and fishing terms. It lacks a loch to act as a reservoir to maintain water levels. Therefore Halladale rods look for rain and spates on the heels of which the sport can come fast and furious. And, just to make the whole thing more interesting, the rule on the Halladale, as on its neighbours, is fly only.

Salmon will be taken as early as April in a normal season but the best months, as on the great majority of northern rivers, are from June to September. The average size of Halladale salmon, at about 7 lb, is quite small, but the numbers of summer salmon and grilse, given that all–important factor of rain, can be excellent. It is not unknown for one angler to take a double number of fish in a day but, there again, it is not too common either!

Whilst the Halladale is a fly-only river, do not imagine that the fly is fished in the sort of conventional manner that would work, say, on a middle-Spey beat. The simple truth is that most of the Halladale is sluggish and, where there is insufficient flow to swim the fly attractively, the fisherman must do something about it. An upstream wind to ruffle the water surface is undoubtedly a great advantage. And if you feel your fly needs to be given a touch more life about it, you gently handline to accelerate your fly across, shooting the retrieved line on the next cast.

Choice of fly may be based entirely on individual whim or on some other factor. For example, many anglers choose the pattern of fly according to the colour of the water. On the Halladale, which flows over peat, the general pattern of a spate is that it will be heavily peat-stained at its height and virtually unfishable to start

*Fishing down a rocky beat on the Helmsdale*

with. Then, on the following day as it falls and begins to clear but still carries a degree of colour, flies such as the Garry Dog and Yellow and Orange come into their own. The water falls and clears further, and a Willie Gunn may prove successful – one with a fairly high proportion of yellow to its black and orange. Next, as spate conditions become something of a memory, good old favourites like the Hairy Mary and the Stoat's Tail can be very useful.

This dependence on spates to produce good fishing becomes more marked the higher you travel up the river. Some fish will squeeze into the lower beats despite low water but on the top beats it is very much a case of no rain, no fish.

Little mention has been made of sea–trout – in truth none at all. The fact is that while they can be caught down in the Halladale's wide estuary there is not much of a run up into the river.

## Access

The Halladale is divided into six beats for fishing. At the present time, some of the beats may be changing hands, so it will be as well to check the information below in future years.

The lower four beats are fished in rotation. Inquiries should be made to the existing agent, who also handles some good if rather remote loch fishing for trout. Contact:

Mrs J. Atkinson
8 Sinclair Street
Thurso
Caithness
*Telephone* 0847 63291

The two uppermost beats are fished by guests of the Forsinard Hotel, which also has some good hill loch fishing for trout. Contact:

Forsinard Hotel
Forsinard
Sutherland
*Telephone* 06417 221

## FORSS

The Forss has fairly extensive headwaters and tributaries, but that part which is of interest to the fisherman is a fairly short section flowing out of Loch Shurrery. The word *forss* is a Norse word for a waterfall and, indeed, the river goes over falls under the Bridge of Forss. The Forss has very slow water in its lowermost mile.

Until recent seasons, the Forss tended to be something of a closed book, in private hands. However, rod fishing is now available and, to make the proposition all the more attractive, netting at the mouth of the river has ceased. The river is now being fished as two four-rod beats, one above and one below the Falls.

Early-season visitors should note that while the Forss enjoys a spring run of fish, those taken in the early months of the season will be found below the Falls, which act as a temperature barrier. Until the water temperature rises into the upper forties, normally in late April, the salmon will ascend no farther. Sport continues through the season with summer grilse and then a late run of salmon.

## Season

11 February to 31 October.

## Access

Full details from:

> Harper's Fly Fishing Services
> The Drill Hall
> Thurso
> Caithness
> *Telephone* 0847 63179

# THURSO

The source of the Thurso is a spring on the high, windswept Knockfin Heights. Its upper course is across deep, peat-covered moorland, over the Strathhalladale granite bedrock and gravel ground down by glaciers of the last Ice Age. This upper river provides the Thurso salmon with a great reserve of spawning and nursery areas.

## Season

11 January to 5 October (best August–September).

## The Beat System

The upper Thurso ends where the river flows into Loch More. It is the section of the river downstream from the loch that forms the significant part of the fishing. This lower section is divided into 13 beats, excluding the private beat known as Lord Thurso's beat, which he keeps for himself, his friends or special visitors.

Beat 1 is used by the Thurso Angling Club. The rest of the numbered beats are fished in rotation by guests who stay at the Ulbster Arms Hotel in Halkirk. Beats are numbered moving upstream. Numbers 1–4 lie between Thurso Bay and Halkirk. Beats 5–9 are from Halkirk up to the junction with the Little River. Beats 10–13, and the private beat, lie between the junction with the Little River and Loch More.

The beats are fished in rotation, moving down two each day. Thus, if you stayed for a week and started on beat 13, you would fish 13, 11, 9, 7, 5 and 3, and, if you stayed for a further week, it would be 12, 10, 8, 6, 4 and 2. Each pool has 8–10 productive pools and in this way overcrowding is avoided and the fishing day is filled.

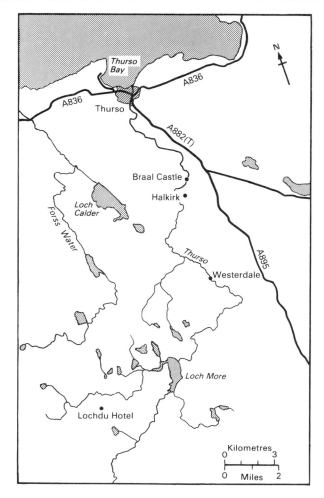

Map 23    *The Thurso*

**Fish**

There may well be salmon in the Thurso during January and February but they are thin on the ground and few fishermen are tempted to make a serious effort, so catches tend to be very few and far between. March sees the start of more serious attempts to catch salmon and, surprisingly, it is often found that it is the upper beats, close to Loch More, that can yield the best sport.

April sees the fishing improve, and it may be that close to 100 salmon will be caught. A good April generally means a good May, with about equal numbers being taken in each month. June tends to be a little betwixt and between, as it is on many Highland rivers. You see, June tends to be a dry month and, without rain and spates to bring in fresh fish, June may find anglers trying to tempt fish that have been in the river for some time. Then comes July, rainfall is that little bit more predictable, and sport gets under way with a bang as summer salmon and grilse pour into the river. These runs will peak and continue through August and September – given rain, of course. To give some idea of the scope of what has gone before, it has been recorded that, in 1974, in the first five days of October for which the river remains open, more than 200 salmon were taken.

Loch More needs special mention. No boat is provided but any angler, whatever his beat, can try his luck on this loch. All fishing is with the fly, as it is on the river. The loch can fish particularly well in June, or it may just be that this is the time when the river, due to a lack of rain, causes anglers to search about for an alternative, and many of the early-running salmon may be in the loch by this time.

## Fishing

This is no fast, tumbling stream, certainly not throughout its entire length. In fact, the fall over 25 miles of river, from Loch More to the sea, is only 300 feet. It is inevitable, therefore, that a number of Thurso beats have a proportion of slow-moving pools. But this is not a problem, particularly if you have decent water heights, perhaps an upstream breeze to ruffle the water, and the knowledge of how such stretches should best be fished if they are to give success.

The standard technique used for fishing slow stretches on the Thurso is backing up. Start at the bottom rather than the top of the pool and cast as long a line as you can at a fairly square angle. In early spring, when the fly should be fished deep, nothing is done for a few seconds while the fly is given time to sink. Then a few yards of line are drawn in by hand. This sets the fly on the move. Then the angler takes two or three paces upstream. This keeps the fly on the move. Then a few more yards are recovered before the angler gently raises his rod, either into a taking salmon or to flick back up into the back cast. Cast square and repeat.

It all sounds quite improbable but those who regularly use the backing-up techniques will champion its effectiveness. Indeed, there have been times and places where backing up has worked so well for me personally that I have insisted, even on those pools with sufficient flow to swim the fly unaided, on fishing the pools

down in the conventional manner, and then immediately pro-
ceeded to back up.

The favourite flies for fishing in early spring, before the water
has risen in temperature to the upper forties, are generally tied on
2-inch or 3-inch tubes in patterns such as the Yellow and Black, the
Orange and Black and the Munro Killer. The modern generation of
long-winged flies are also proving their worth with some Thurso
anglers. The Tadpole and Collie Dog are the best known of this
type. For some unknown reason, the Tadpole will take fish at
the lowest temperatures while experience has shown virtually
wherever they have been tried that the Collie Dog is best held in
reserve until the water temperature has risen above 40 degrees.

Later in the season, when the water temperature has steadied into
the fifties and more, and fishermen are seeking their sport with
floating lines or, for a minority, the intermediate or sink-tip,
smaller doubles and long-shanked trebles become the thing. The
most used sizes on the Thurso are 8 and 10 for summer salmon and
grilse. Standard patterns such as the Stoat's Tail, Munro Killer,
Tosh, Hairy Mary and Garry can all work well.

Much has been said of the necessity for rainfall and, while it is
true that the reservoir of Loch More can maintain water height over
an extended period, a lack of water in June does tend to favour the
lowermost beat, which, as has been mentioned, is association
water. Given a dry summer, this stretch below Halkirk can yield
really excellent sport. Day tickets may be available if not required
by members.

## Access

The Thurso is just about the only salmon river of significant size
that falls under individual ownership, management, and therefore
letting. All guests fishing the river must stay at the Ulbster Arms
Hotel in Halkirk. Little surprise that this is under the same
ownership as the river! Contact:

> Ulbster Arms Hotel
> Halkirk
> Caithness
> *Telephone* 084 783 206

> Thurso Fisheries Ltd
> *Telephone* 0847 63134

# 8 Orkney and Shetland

Both these chains of islands have long enjoyed a reputation for great sport, not only for perfect wild brown trout but also for sea-trout. It is said that the sea-trout are always present around the Shetland Islands, but they tend to concentrate in the sea lochs, known as voes, during the autumn, which makes this a recognisable 'best time'. But sea-trout are suffering and, dare I say it, so long as the thinking of national angling associations is fixed firmly on salmon and trout, the future may not be very rosy. There is, however, one light on the horizon. There is a strong possibility that at least part of the sea-trout's problems are the same as those being experienced by the enormous populations of sea birds in these coastal waters. It is that their prey, mainly sandeels, is being harvested by man to feed the fishmeal factories. Birds attract great interest and protection on a national level, and we can at least hope that, if something is done to help protect their food, it will, in turn, help the sea-trout. On the other side of the coin, however, it will do nothing to limit the number of seals which, despite their recent traumas, still exist in populations that fishermen find alarming.

## ORKNEY

There are two lochs on Orkney where sea-trout are regularly caught. These are Lochs Stenness and Harray. Loch of Stenness lies 3 miles from Stromness and 12 miles from Kirkwall. Loch Harray is fairly close to Stenness, being 4 miles from Stromness and 11 miles from Kirkwall. I do not think that it would be all that unfair to say that nobody regularly sets out on either Stenness or Harray with the clear intention of catching sea-trout, certainly not in the general run of Orcadian fishing. Remember that these are lochs whose reputations as producers of wild brown trout attract anglers from all over the world. And so the bulk of the sea-trout are taken when the boat-borne loch fisherman is fishing his team of wet flies for trout – flies chosen from such local favourites as the Black Pennell, Butcher, Grouse and Claret, Invicta, Ke-He, Loch Ordie, various Palmers and Zulus, Peter Ross, Wickham's Fancy, and so on. The time when you would most expect close encounters with

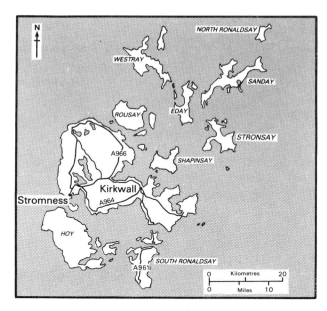

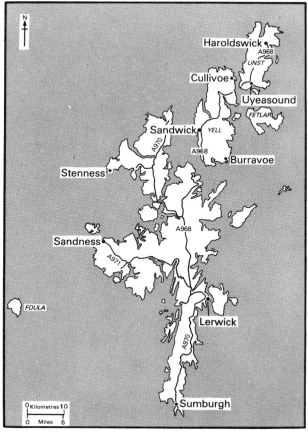

Map 24   *Orkney and Shetland*

sea-trout on either of the lochs is in March and April, and then again from July through to late October.

When fishing specifically for sea-trout, most Orcadians think in terms of the sea. Well, perhaps not so much the sea as inlets and bays where freshwater streams run into salt to form brackish water. Wading perhaps chest-high and casting out a long, thin tandem lure to search the fringes of the deep beds of seaweed can produce an electric take and exhilarating sport with the freshest of fresh sea-trout. Besides the mainland, the eastern shores of the island of Hoy are a favourite area for saltwater sea-trout fishing on Orkney.

## Access

Most of the fishing on Orkney is controlled and cared for by the Orkney Angling Association. Membership is voluntary, and you can fish some waters without permission or payment, but it is my view that the sort of person who would fish Orkney without joining the association would also probably steal from his mother.

*A fine loch-caught 4 lb sea-trout, showing the spade-like tail that distinguishes it from a salmon*

For details of the fishing on Orkney, contact the Tourist Information Officer, Kirkwall, Orkney.


## SHETLAND

Mainlanders might regard the Shetland Islands as the northern outpost of the far-flung British Isles. Many Shetlanders, however, view things rather differently and assert that they are, in fact, the southernmost outpost of Scandinavia. One hundred islands braving the harsh North Atlantic and caught in the debatable ground of nationality. Until fairly recent times, they were remote and unspoilt, but all that has changed. Texas Tea, Black Gold – call it what you will – when oil was discovered in the North Sea these islands were transformed. And, it is said, the developments that came on the heels of the discovery of oil have done nothing at all for Shetland's legendary sea-trout fishing. Indeed, they are often blamed as one of the principal causes for its decline. But this does not deny the fact that, if no longer so numerous, there are still sea-trout and sport to be had.

Sea-trout in Shetland spells saltwater fishing. You may choose to spin, in which case you could be well advised to follow the Shetland practice of attaching a long, thin lash of mackerel to the treble of your spinner. An alternative with the lash of mackerel is to mount it on a Pennell tackle, with two hooks in tandem, and fish it on conventional fly tackle, though it does require a certain skill in casting and it is best to use a good long rod.

Alternatively, you may fish more conventional sea-trout flies. Tandem dressings of such patterns as the Teal, Blue and Silver can work well. It is presumed that such demons and terrors are mistaken for small fish or sandeels. But you can also catch a share of sea-trout on standard sea-trout flies such as the Peter Ross and the Blae and Black. It is amazing, perhaps, that such small flies are taken with such gusto. And I would like to try a Shrimp Fly, to see if this would produce a take.


### Season and Access

The sea-trout season in Shetland extends from 25 February to the end of October. Beside the sea-trout, the Shetland Islands also offer excellent loch fishing for trout. Most of the mainland waters are controlled by the Shetland Anglers' Association, which charges a very small fee for a season ticket. Contact:

Andrew Miller
3 Gladstone Terrace
Lerwick
Shetland

Incidentally, the association's waters now include Spiggie Loch. This is a good sea-trout fishery, as well as being Shetland's largest loch.

The best times for sea-trout are from late March through to the start of May, with sport then picking up again in the months of July, August and September. It is said that until you have caught a 6-pounder in Shetland's sea you really don't know what sea-trout fishing is about.

Since the oil industry came to Shetland access has improved immensely. Besides the car ferry from Aberdeen, regular flights arrive and leave from Sumburgh. For full details of accommodation and fishing, contact the Tourist Information Office, Lerwick, Shetland.

# 9 The North-East

## WESTER

The Wester is one of those waters which tend to be left out of most fishing guides. I can only imagine that this is because most guides are prepared with salmon fishermen in mind. It is true that the Wester River and Loch yield only a few salmon, but, on the other hand, they are a good sea-trout fishery, perhaps the best in Caithness.

The loch, which may be fished either from boat or bank, is fairly small and shallow, certainly when compared with the great sea-trout lochs of the west coast, but can yield good sport, with sea-trout to an average weight of about 1½ lb, and an occasional 4- or 5-pounder to lucky rods. The river also fishes well for sea-trout and offers an attractive alternative to the loch on days of blustery winds.

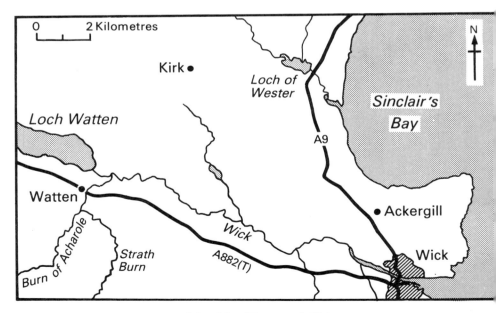

Map 25   *Wester and Wick*

**Season**

1 April to 31 October.

**Fishing**

If fishing the loch for the first time, you might like to make a start with a three-fly cast with, say, a Peter Ross on the point, a Grouse and Claret on the middle, and a Black Pennell or a Soldier Palmer on the bob. These four flies have proved their worth to generations of trout and sea-trout fishermen on a host of Scottish waters. Note should be made that the Wester is fly-only.

In loch fishing for sea-trout careful working of the top dropper, the bob fly, on the surface of the waves can be a deadly technique. A long rod of 11 or 12 feet in carbon fibre makes the control of the furrowing fly all the easier.

**Access**

Permission for boat and bank fishing is available from:

C. Dunnet
Auckhorn
Lyth
Caithness
*Telephone* 095583 208

**WICK**

The Wick is the second biggest river in Caithness. Even so, it is quite narrow and rather similar to the Halladale in that it has long stretches of sluggish water, which many anglers choose to fish with a worm. Indeed, between Watten and Wick, a distance of some 10 miles through quite rich agricultural land, the fall is only 10 feet. As you will appreciate, a fall of 1 foot per mile is hardly conducive to creating a strong flow!

**Season**

11 February to 21 October (best May–October).

## Fish and Fishing

Despite what some might see as the rather unattractive appearance of the river, it regularly produces more than 400 salmon and, in some seasons, as many as 600 salmon have been recorded. The first of these may be caught in March or April, but it is really through the summer months, given rain, and up to the close of the season that the Wick shows its best. Note that point about rain. Heavy rain is required to bring in fish and in a dry summer the river can fade away to little more than a trickle.

Summer months can see good runs of grilse averaging about 5 lb in weight, but the Wick is also capable of producing salmon of 20 lb.

The river is one of the few in the north that allows the use of worm and spinner as well as fly. Worm fishing is allowed from 1 April to 30 September. Fly fishers who are prepared to impart life to their fly by handlining or backing up or both may account for approximately half the salmon taken from the Wick each season. In

*Inviting lies at Westerdales on the Thurso*

summer, with flies of size 8 or 10 in patterns such as the Stoat's Tail, Hairy Mary and Munro Killer, particularly when there is a good breeze to ruffle the water, backing up can work very well indeed.

As to spinning lures, perhaps because the flow is sluggish Devon minnows are the popular choice. The black-and-gold and the brown-and-gold are both popular, as are the black-and-orange and the black-and-yellow.

## Access

Wick Angling Association controls the fishing between Loch Watten and Wick. There are more than twenty pools on this stretch. Permits are available from the following:

Hugo Ross Fishing Tackle
Breadalbane Street
Wick

The Sports Shop
High Street
Wick

Camps Sport Centre
Camps

## BERRIEDALE

The Berriedale and its close neighbour the Langwell actually join together at the village of Berriedale, some 300 yards above the estuary. Of the two, the Berriedale is most significant in terms of size as well as salmon. The Langwell produces only a handful of fish, but the 20-mile-long Berriedale may show 60 or 70 salmon in a normal season and perhaps a dozen sea-trout. The average size of salmon and grilse in the Berriedale is small at about 5 lb but, if fished for appropriately, fish of this size can give good sport. As always, good fishing is entirely dependent on rain and spates.

## Season

11 February to 31 October (best July–September).

## Access

Weekly permits may be available. Apply to:

The Factor
Langwell Estate
Berriedale
*Telephone* 05935 237

## HELMSDALE

The Helmsdale is a fantastic salmon river. It is undoubtedly the heaviest producer of salmon in Sutherland and, indeed, in the north of Scotland. The fact of the matter is, however, that the best of the fishing, certainly at the peak times of the season, is strictly preserved. The six owners of the river act as a co-operative in that they pool and share their resources. Their holding is divided into twelve beats, six above the Falls and six below. Each estate can fish two rods a day, and they decide whether to fish together on one beat or separately on two. And the beats rotate each day so that, in a week, each rod has at least the opportunity to fish the entire river. And after April, once the runs of salmon and grilse have really started in earnest – well St Peter might find it hard to get a rod on the Helmsdale!

There are possibilities, nevertheless, of taking a beat in the months up to April, and there is a stretch of association fishing

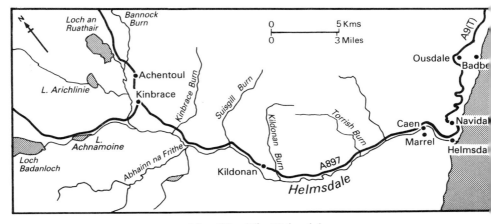

Map 26　*The Helmsdale*

above the estuary. So let me take a closer look at access and sport on this magnificent river.

## Season

11 January to 30 September.

## The Beats

The beat system on the Helmsdale is divided into six upper and six lower beats, the dividing point between upper and lower being the Kildonan Falls. This is not just a demarcation point because, where the early-season fishing is concerned, no salmon will ascend these falls until the water temperature exceeds 42°F. Therefore early-season fishermen ignore the upper beats. Later on in the year, when fish are over the falls, besides the fact that the beats will rotate at 8 p.m. anyway, greater consideration has to be given to whether the fishing is likely to be best above or below. Say the two rods have Beat 1 below and Beat 1 above. They may decide that at a certain state of the tide they will fare better on the below beat, and later they will jump in a car and race up to their above beat. Of course, their opinions may differ, and then one rod can fish the above beat and the other the below beat.

## Fish

There is a good chance of catching a salmon on the opening day of the Helmsdale season. Then again, it is not uncommon for the river to be frozen over at any time during January and February. No problem – many a successful early-season Helmsdale fisherman has started the day by helping his gillie to break ice to clear a pool, and some will even argue that, by stirring up the comatosed fish, this can even improve the fishing chances.

Salmon should have ascended the falls in the last week of March. This coincides with the start of a build-up in sheer numbers entering the river. April and May are normally excellent. Then come runs of summer grilse, which normally start in June, peak in July, and then fall away in August.

Catch figures for the Helmsdale are as hard to find as anywhere, but somebody let the cat out of the bag ten years ago when it was reported that Beat 4 above had enjoyed a best day of 31 fish, a best week of 94 and a season's total of 599.

**Fishing**

The Helmsdale is fly-only. In the opening months of the season, before the water temperature has risen above 50°F, most fishing will be done with a 15-foot carbon rod, sinking line, fairly stout leader and a big tube fly. Favoured patterns will include the Willie Gunn, Garry Dog, Black and Orange, Black and Yellow, Collie Dog and Tadpole.

In summer, while some may choose to continue with their 15-footers, others will change to a rather shorter, lighter and handier rod to fish the floating line in sizes from 8 down to 12, with black flies such as the Stoat's Tail, the Tosh, and so on often doing well. A friend of mine who is lucky enough to fish the Helmsdale at its peak time tells me that he takes virtually all his summer salmon and grilse on a tiny Silver Stoat tube fly, armed with a deadly little outpoint treble.

No discussion of Helmsdale fishing would be complete without a mention of the technique known as dibbling. This is a refined technique for fishing a dropper, and mainly to be used on the fast, broken headstreams of pools where salmon congregate in low-water summer conditions.

The dropper is tied in quite high up the leader, say 6 feet above the point fly on a 10-foot leader, and the dropper length may be as much as 8 inches. This is in contrast to the standard dropper rig for salmon where the dropper is attached about 4 feet from the point fly and is only a couple of inches in length.

The dropper is made to dibble across the water surface, scratching away in the surface of the stream and cutting a wake. A short line and a long but sensitive rod make the technique all the easier, and the fisherman must be prepared to keep plugging away. It is one of the features of dibbling that a salmon or grilse is just as likely to take on the sixth or sixtieth cast over the same stream as it is on the first.

One other feature of dibbling is that so many of the salmon that are risen are not subsequently hooked. In fact, you can reckon yourself something of an expert in the technique when you hook one out of every two salmon you rise.

Popular flies for dibbling are often tied on double hooks and fished one size larger than the point fly. A choice of pattern could be made from the Elver Fly, Shrimp Fly, Garry, Willie Gunn or Stoat's Tail, among others.

Finally, while there are some fairly sluggish stretches on the Helmsdale, such as between Baddywood and Kilearnan Bridge on Beat 4 below, they can be very productive if a combination of backing up and handlining is employed to give the fly movement and the semblance of life.

## Access

Access to private beats on the Helmsdale is strictly limited, and your only chance is in the early months of the season. It is undoubtedly a very great help to know the friend of a friend who may be giving up his week. Otherwise, inquiries might be made to:

Colin Taylor
Rods and Guns
Fountain Square
Brora
*Telephone* 0408 21323

Alternatively, there is the angling association's water at the village of Helmsdale. There is about one mile of fishing and it can produce good salmon fishing from the start of the season and right on through, as well as showing excellent sport with sea-trout. Day tickets are available from:

Alex Jappy
Fish Merchant
The Harbour
Helmsdale

## BRORA

The two main tributaries of the Brora rise in the Borrobol Forest and Ben Armine Forest. These tributaries are the Blackwater and the Upper Brora, and they join at Balnacoil, after which the river flows on into 4-mile-long Loch Brora. The lower Brora flows out of the loch on a three-mile journey to the sea.

## Season

1 February to 15 October (best February–May).

## Fish

The early runs of salmon into the Brora coincide with the start of the season to ensure that the season will normally get off to a running start, with perhaps 100 fish taken in February. March can

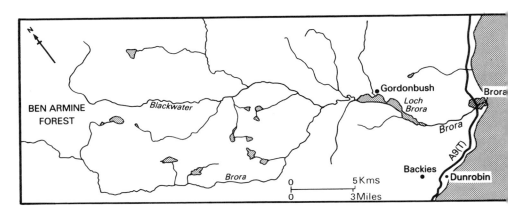

Map 27   *The Brora*

be equally productive, and this spring sport with early fish can continue through to May. In recognition of this fact, and because spring runs tend to be few and far between at a national level in the modern age, we say that the Brora's 'best times' are from February to May. This should not blind us, however, to the fact that the Brora continues to show excellent sport through the summer. Given rainfall and reasonable water levels, the summer salmon and grilse fishing of June and July can be excellent.

The Brora can also show excellent sport with sea–trout from June onwards.

In addition to the formal closed season, various other limitations have been put on Brora anglers as conservation measures. For example, all sea-trout caught before May – or, better still, June – should be returned to the river. The season on the Blackwater tributary, because it is important for spawning, closes on 1 September, and no hen fish is to be killed on any other beat after 15 September. All sportsmen should applaud such measures.

The lower river produces the salmon in the opening weeks of the season, but soon the fish are populating the loch and then thrusting on to make the upper river the most productive for the rest of the season.

The lower river is owned by Sutherland Estates on the south bank and Gordonbush on the north bank. The loch is jointly owned by the two estates and fishing is allowed from the start of May. Hotels have boats on the loch as well as the estates. Above the loch, the upper Brora is owned by the Gordonbush Estate, as is the Blackwater, but the Ben Armine Water is owned by Sutherland Estates.

*A classic February springer from the Helmsdale*

## Fishing

All the Sutherland rivers are fly-only, and the Brora is no exception. Indeed, many of the most effective modern fly patterns – such as the Willie Gunn, the Pilkington, and so on – have evolved in this area. Both the long-winged Collie Dog and the Tadpole are also justifiably popular for early-season fishing. Often these are tied on large tubes, up to 3-inches long, and armed with a treble hook. As an alternative, and a very popular one, wire-bodied flies are used a great deal. Their design is based upon the lines of a double Waddington shank except that rather heavier, stainless-steel wire is used.

The generally accepted rule in cold-water early-season salmon fishing is to fish the fly deep and as slowly as possible but, on the Brora and other Highland rivers having a spring run, more and more anglers are discovering that even early on in the season salmon will rise to take a big fly fishing close to the surface. Using either a Collie or Tadpole tied, perhaps, with a 6-inch trailing wing on a 2-inch brass tube and presenting it off a floating line breaks all the traditions and conventions of salmon fishing but, my goodness, how well it can work! I would, however, tend to see this as an alternative to rather than a replacement of the more traditional style, and to be fished in a spirit of partnership rather than competition.

Whether fishing sunk or floating line, because of the size of the fly and the task in hand a good and powerful 15-footer proves itself just the thing for this relatively heavy early-season work. As May fades to June, the rod chosen may be that little bit shorter, perhaps, and certainly more sensitive. For now sees the start of floating-line tactics in their widely accepted form, with small flies from 8 down to 12 on double or long-shanked treble hooks. Popular patterns now are the Hairy Mary, the Munro Killer, the Stoat's Tail and the Tosh.

Loch Brora provides excellent sport with sea-trout as well as salmon, and the Kenny's Killer is a great favourite for sea-trout. On the loch, fish a long rod and light line, choosing a team of wet flies from such favourites as Peter Ross, Dunkeld, Mallard and Claret, Dark Mackerel, Black Pennell, and so on. In a good height of wave the heavily hackled Loch Ordie is an excellent fly to trip through the wave tops in the top dropper or bob position.

**Access**

The estuary and a tidal stretch of about half a mile can be fished free of charge for salmon and sea-trout from 1 May through to the close of the season. It is particularly good for sea-trout, but salmon can also be caught.

Fishing on the river and its tributaries may be available from either of the two estates:

Sutherland Estates
Golspie
Sutherland
*Telephone* 04083 3268

Gordonbush Estate
Brora
Sutherland
*Telephone* 0408 21323

The loch is fished by boat and the fishing can be excellent. A boat can be booked from the Sutherland Estates (see above) or the Loch Brora Angling Club. Hotels with boats are as follows:

Sutherland Arms Hotel, *telephone* 0408 21209
Royal Marine Hotel, *telephone* 0408 21252
Links Hotel, *telephone* 0408 21225

Another boat is available through Colin Taylor, the relatively new owner of what used to be Rob Wilson's shop in Fountain Square, who maintains the tradition of being a mine of information on fishing and stocking all that any fisherman might require:

Rods and Guns
Fountain Square
Brora
Sutherland
*Telephone* 0408 21373

## FLEET

Because of the close proximity of internationally renowned salmon rivers the Fleet is often ignored. It is a small river. The fisherman need concern himself only with about 9 miles of it, and this flows into the tidal waters of Loch Fleet. But from June onwards, given decent water levels, the river can fish well for salmon and sea-trout and, should the river suffer from a summer drought, the loch continues to provide sport.

Flies for the Fleet seldom need to be large. Sizes 8 down to 12 in a pattern such as the Stoat's Tail are very useful for grilse and salmon. Note that this is a fly-only river. Many sea-trout are taken on the Teal, Blue and Silver, the Dunkeld and the Zulu.

### Season

1 June to 15 October.

### Access

Access is available to the river through the Rogart Angling Club. Two beats are available, but access is limited to one day per week on one, and two days per week on the other. In addition, the day is divided into three sessions. Where visitors are concerned, they pay a joining fee to the club, and then an extra charge for each session that they take.

Membership and permits are handled through:

Rogart Hotel
Rogart
by Lairg
Sutherland
*Telephone* 040 84 353

# 10 The Kyle of Sutherland

The Kyle of Sutherland is really an enormous estuary, a deep, 14-mile-long slash into the coast of Sutherland. It penetrates inland from the coast to beyond Bonar Bridge. It is, in fact, estuary to four major rivers: Shin, Oykel, Cassley and Carron. All these rivers employ the fly-only rule and they all have early salmon followed by summer salmon and grilse runs. A similar style of fishing is used on all four rivers and the same flies are popular, so the following notes apply to all of them.

**Season**

11 January to 30 September.

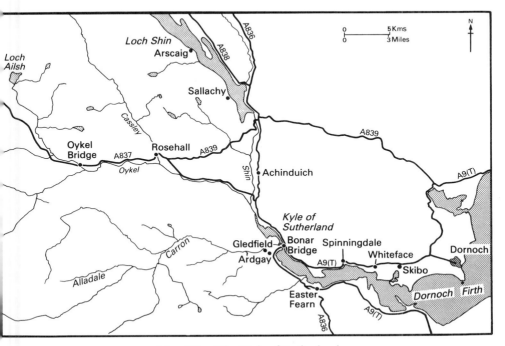

Map 28   *The Kyle of Sutherland*

**Fishing**

All the Kyle of Sutherland rivers get off to an early start, and there is some local competition to see who will take the first fish of the season. In 1988 the Carron produced a salmon on the opening day of the season and on the following day, 12 January, another was taken from the Cassley. Early fish indeed and, as things turned out, the first two salmon of the season for the whole of Britain.

At this early stage of the season the big articulated flies, either tubes or wire-shanked, are the thing and the basis of the early-season technique is to fish them deep and slow. Perhaps the most popular patterns are the Black and Yellow, the Garry, the Pilkington and the tremendously popular Willie Gunn.

As an alternative, more and more fishermen are discovering the seductive properties of long-winged flies such as the Collie Dog and the Tadpole. And, what is more, besides the fact that these flies prove very attractive fished in the conventional sunk-line manner, they are also capable of moving fish even when fished off a floating line, and in February and March. Incidentally, although I cannot for the life of me suggest why it should be so, experience seems to suggest that while the Tadpole will work at virtually any temperature the Collie is best reserved until the water temperature exceeds 40°F. A long-winged fly shimmering across the current and a cold-water salmon showing in the take – but, as I have said elsewhere, it is a method to be fished perhaps in partnership rather than competition with more standard tactics with flies such as the Willie Gunn.

Heavy flies and lines require long, powerful rods. I regard a 15-footer as a virtual minimum length for satisfactory sunk-line fishing, and am often glad to make use of an extra foot or two to ease the burden of roll and Spey casting. Incidentally, whether you stick with the now rather outmoded overhead cast or have taken to employing the Spey casts, always start with an initial roll cast to bring the line to the water surface or you may overstrain the most powerful rod, or end up with a fly dangling from your ear.

Then comes late spring leading into summer. The water temperature rises above 50 degrees and fishermen everywhere will be laying aside their heavy tackle to turn to more sensitive small-fly tackle and techniques. Personally, I seldom go below 14 feet unless I am specifically fishing for grilse, when I will perhaps choose a light 13-footer or a single-handed rod of about 11 feet. All the old favourites are brought out of the fly box for summer use, including such as the Hairy Mary, the Munro Killer and Jeannie, but there are those who feel that if a salmon will take anything it will probably take a Stoat's Tail in its funereal garb. Others say that the pattern

*Well hooked in the kype, this cock salmon fell to the Waddington*

is not important, and that size is the thing. On this point one interesting factor seems to be emerging. It used to be said that a size 6 should be considered the standard for summer use, with smaller flies tried only if the fish showed no interest. In recent seasons, however, and not just on these Kyle rivers, catch figures tend to reveal that the 6 is losing favour and the great bulk of summer salmon and grilse are falling to sizes 8, 10 and 12 or, at the other end of the scale, small Collies and Tadpoles, 'small' meaning perhaps a 1-inch tube with a 3-inch wing. Make of it what you will!

## SHIN

The Shin is the northernmost of the four principal salmon rivers of the Kyle. It has been hydroised and is subject to controlled compensation flow. It does, however, still produce salmon in excellent quantity and quality.

Shin fishing begins at the start of the season, with virtually all activity being centred on the lower river, below the Falls of Shin. This stretch is very rocky and the water often runs clear to make exciting and highly visual sport. But the Shin's spring fishing is not what it once was, and the spring run, it has to be said, does not compare with its neighbours'. Sport picks up steadily, with May normally proving to be the best spring month. It will be June before fish ascend the Falls of Shin, which involves a considerable leap, and then move up to congregate below the dam at Lairg. July is the peak summer month with the beats either side of the Falls faring well, and then the sport is virtually over by the end of August.

**Access**

The fishing on the Shin is very popular and access hard to gain, but the Sutherland Arms leases beats at certain times on both the upper and lower river. Contact:

Sutherland Arms Hotel
Lairg
Sutherland
*Telephone* 0549 2291

**OYKEL**

The Oykel is widely regarded as the jewel in the crown of Kyle rivers, producing well over 2,000 salmon in the 1988 season. More than 1,700 of these fish came from the lower river beats.

It remains a spate river, having escaped the attentions of the Hydro Board. It rises on the distant slopes of Ben More Assynt and flows a short distance before entering Loch Ailsh, which has a good reputation for sea-trout. The next part of the river is surprisingly slow-flowing but then, below Oykel Bridge, the Oykel is joined by its major tributary, the Einaig, and this pushes on the pace.

Salmon will be caught in January if the river is not completely frozen over, but February is normally better. These fish will all be taken below the Rock Pool on the lower river, which acts as a temperature pool. Once the water temperature rises to 42°F, however, normally in early March, the fish push on farther. But they will not pass over the Oykel Falls until the water temperature reaches 50°. There are also falls on the Einag, which cause the same stoppage for fish running this tributary. It will be late May in a normal season before either of the falls is ascended by running fish. On the upper river, sport now begins and continues through June, July and August, with most fish being caught in September – though, by then, they have been in the river for a while and may be past their best. These upper beats, fished by guests of the Oykel Bridge Hotel, can produce about 150 salmon on average, though in 1988 they produced just short of 400 in the season.

## Access

As you would expect on such a fine river, access is far from easy to find. The lower river is privately owned and fished as four rotating beats. If you wish to have your name added at the end of an already long waiting list, contact Lower Oykel Fishing, Rosehall, by Lairg, Sutherland. Beats on the upper river, which are also hard to get, are handled through the Oykel Bridge Hotel (*telephone* 054 984 218).

Part of the upper river and Loch Ailsh, with its reputation for sea-trout, are owned by the Assynt Estate. This is well over towards the west coast, and the beat and loch are fished by guests staying at the estate's hotel, the Inver Lodge Hotel, Lochinver (*telephone* 057 14 496). This hotel also has the fishing on the Kirkaig and upper Inver.

## CASSLEY

The Cassley has had its headwaters tapped by the Hydro Board and so spates tend to be short-lived. Therefore the Cassley does tend to experience a lot of low water. On the other hand, the lower river has been cleverly improved to cope.

One or two salmon may be caught on the lower Cassley in January and February. Fish will stay in the lower river, below Achness Falls – the Rosehall beat – until the water temperature reaches 52°F, normally some time in June. By then 200 and more salmon will have been taken off the Rosehall beat. The best summer month for grilse at Rosehall is generally July and, by then, the upper river is also fishing well. Sea-trout are taking well on the entire length of the river by this time.

The owner of the Rosehall beat is the distinguished fishery consultant and writer Neil Graesser. Besides running his beat as a model of all that is best in fishery management, he is also the inventor of the long-winged Tadpole and a staunch champion of

*Short casts and steady feet; salmon can lie in surprisingly fast flowing runs*

the Collie Dog. Even in summer he will fish such flies, albeit in relatively shorter lengths, and he always fishes a dropper. Popular patterns include the Hairy Mary, the Stoat, and so on.

**Access**

Rosehall is managed and let either through Neil Graesser (*telephone* 054984 202) or from the Achness Hotel, Rosehall, by Lairg, Sutherland (*telephone* 054984 239).

Upper Cassley beats are handled by Bell Ingram, Estate Agents, Bonar Bridge, Sutherland (*telephone* 08632 632).

**CARRON**

The Carron flows north to enter the south side of the Kyle at Bonar Bridge. Despite an enormous catchment area, the river rises and falls very quickly during a spate, due to part of its headwaters being diverted for the hydro. However, the early-season flow is sustained by snow-melt from the mountains on the catchment area, and this is a great aid to Carron fishing during February, March and April, and often into May.

Salmon may be caught in January up as far as Gledfield, which acts as a temperature pool. Fish hold at Gledfield until the water temperature rises to 42°F, then fish run on to the upper beats, followed by sea-trout from June onwards. Runs of summer salmon and grilse tend to forge on to the upper reaches. And so, as on so many rivers, if you could pick your places and times to fish for salmon, it would be the lower beats up to Gledfield from the earliest part of the season through to April, and then on to the upper river for June, July and August to take a mixed bag of sea-trout, grilse and summer salmon.

## Access

Access is strictly limited as the entire river is in private hands. There are lengthy waiting lists. R. MacLeod and Son of Tain handle the Gledfield beat – *telephone* 0549 2291.

## KYLE OF SUTHERLAND

Finally, the tidal waters of the Kyle itself should never be over-looked. It can produce excellent sport, particularly with sea-trout, which are best approached by boat, though you can fish from the bank. The fly-only rule in force on all the Kyle rivers applies only to certain areas, generally at the mouths of the four rivers, where fish tend to congregate, particularly if the rivers are flowing low. In other parts of the Kyle spinning may be allowed.

## Access

The sea-trout fishing is controlled by the Kyle of Sutherland Angling Club. Permits can be obtained either from R. MacLeod and Son of Tain (*telephone* 0549 2291) or from B. Knott, the newsagent at Ardgay (*telephone* 08632 682). Either of these sources will also be able to advise on hiring one of the many boats that are available in the area.

# 11 Alness, Conon and Beauly

## ALNESS

This relatively small Easter Ross river runs the 10 miles from Loch Morie to the sea – or, to be more precise, the Cromarty Firth. A great amount of work has been done to improve the river, the most important of which for the river's overall benefit was undoubtedly the dam at the bottom end of Loch Morie. With the loch full, water levels in the river can be maintained at an attractive fishing height for two weeks, by which time one may hope to have had more rain. Any fisherman who has fished in summer drought conditions will appreciate the great benefits that such a dam offers.

### Season

11 February to 31 October (best July–October).

### Fish and Fishing

It is not unknown for an odd fish or two to be taken down at the lowest end of the river as early as January and February. April sees numbers growing, and a good proportion of these fish will forge on to the middle and upper reaches. But sport in April and May is

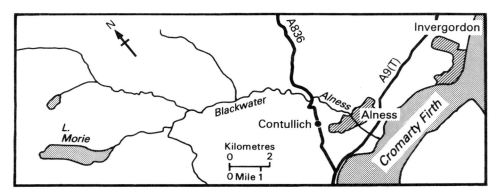

Map 29   *The Alness*

little more than a foretaste of what sport will be like when July ushers in the major runs of summer fish, building to a peak in September and October.

The Alness is not quite fly-only in that, while spinning is never allowed, a worm can be used on some stretches, but only with a fly rod and reel.

Those who fish the fly may choose from established favourites such as the Hairy Mary, the Silver Stoat, and so on, for summer sport with salmon and grilse as well as sea-trout, and then, as the water cools, switch to larger tubes such as a Black and Yellow, a Willie Gunn or a Garry Dog.

## Access

The river is virtually divided between an estate and an angling club, thus giving good scope for access.

Novar Estates have six rotating beats in addition to the Home Beat. In the season of 1988 the rotating beats alone produced just

*The perfect pair – silvery white from the sea*

over 400 salmon. The Coul Lodge Hotel takes one of the rotating beats and inquiries should be made by telephone on 0997 21487. For the other rotating beats contact Novar Estates at Evanton (*telephone* 0349 830208).

Alness Angling Club's permits are handled by

Pattersons Ironmongers
The High Street
Alness
*Telephone* 0349 882286

## CONON AND BLACKWATER

The Conon is the largest of the Ross-shire rivers and is fed by four tributaries – Blackwater, Bran, Meigg and Orin. The tributaries run over peat ground before becoming swift rivers in their own right. They eventually join where steep-sided glens give way to a soft arable vale, and the lower Conon flows on to the Cromarty Firth at Dingwall.

Nine dams have been built on the Conon and its tributaries. And the North of Scotland Hydroelectric Board did not stop there. Pipelines and aqueducts feed Conon water to six power stations.

### Season

26 January to 30 September (best June–August).

### Fish and Fishing

The fairly immediate effect of the hydro development scheme seems to be the fading of the early-season salmon runs. So the period from the opening of the season through to April is not likely to produce more than a handful of fish. May is often better than the preceding months put together, but it is in June that sport really gets under way with returning salmon and grilse. Numbers peak in July and the runs then fade as August lengthens.

Spinning is allowed at certain times on the Conon, with wooden Devon minnows and that great attractor the Toby spoon. Black and gold are popular colours for either lure. Bait, however – be it worm, shrimp or prawn – is not allowed.

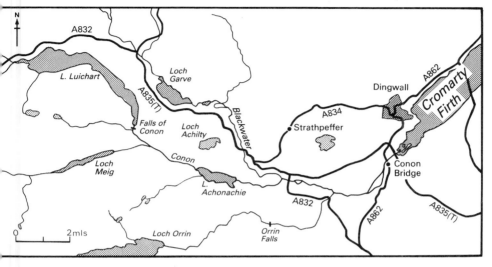

Map 30    *Conon and Blackwater*

## Access

To describe access to the Conon and its tributary the Blackwater is no simple task. You really have to understand something of the politics of the thing but, there again, I have no intention of writing a political book. Therefore let me just say who has what.

Loch Achonachie Angling Club has purchased the upper Conon and Blackwater and also has access to loch fishing. Their water on the upper Blackwater comes down as far as the Falls of Rogie. And their agent for the fishing, half of which they make available to visitors, is:

John MacMillan
Newsagent
The Square
Strathpeffer
Easter Ross
*Telephone* 0997 21346

Below the Falls of Rogie is the middle beat. This is privately owned, but fishing may be available and inquiries can be made to:

Smiths Gore
The Square
Fochabers
Moray
*Telephone* 0343 820213

The bottom beat on the Blackwater is also privately owned but, once again, fishing may be available and inquiries should be made to:

Finlayson Hughes
45 Church Street
Inverness
*Telephone* 0463 224243

The Lower Conon, the famed Brahan beats, have been sold and timeshared.


## BEAULY

The river that we recognize as the Beauly has various names throughout its length. Loch Affric is right up at the top of the system and out of it a small stream flows into Loch Benevean, the outflow of which is the Affric river. The Affric becomes the Glass just upstream of the Fasnakyle power station. The Cannich then joins the Glass and the united two are then joined by the Farrar. From that point on the river is known as the Beauly throughout its length to the salt water of the Beauly Firth.

The Beauly system has been harnessed for the production of hydroelectricity. This has some disadvantages and, it has to be said, perhaps some advantages as well. For example, floods on the Glass used to be devastating and quite literally a risk to life and limb for the local inhabitants.


### Season

11 February to 15 October (best June–October for salmon, April and July–September for sea-trout).


### Fish and Fishing

The tributary rivers are all salmon streams of note in their own right. The Glass can fish very well from mid-July to season's close. Seven of its beats are owned by Lovat Estates, and Struy Estate has one. The upper Farrar tends to be maintained as something of a sanctuary by Lovat Estates, in order to provide an unmolested spawning and nursery ground, but the lower Farrar, owned jointly by the Struy Estate and Culligran Estate, is actively fished and shows fair numbers of salmon and grilse.

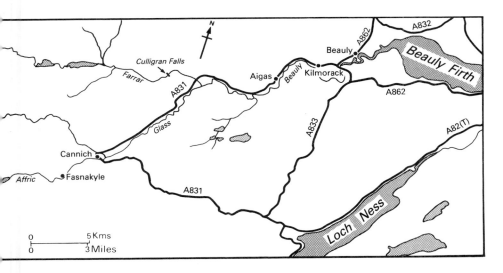

Map 31   *The Beauly*

On the Beauly itself two dams have been erected, at Aigas and Kilmorack.

The best of the Beauly fishings lie below these dams. From Kilmorack downstream, almost to tidal waters, the river is owned by the Lovat Estates and divided into three beats. These beats are the Falls, Home and Downie. Each is fished by four rods. Other Beauly beats include the Aigas and Eskadale beats, both of which lie above Aigas dam and below the confluence with the Farrar.

Some salmon are taken below Kilmorack Dam before April, and generally on big tube flies such as the Willie Gunn or the Garry, but the best of the fishing is from July through to the end of October, though the fish are somewhat coloured in the closing weeks. Fish will not be caught above the dams and in the tributaries until the end of May or early June. Even then, June tends not to be a great month on salmon rivers, and it will be the first spate in July that really gets things moving.

There is a stretch of association water on the lowermost stretch of the Beauly, which again is owned by the Lovat Estates. It can be particularly good for sea-trout fishing, as can the Downie beat higher up. Indeed, the Beauly enjoys excellent runs of sea-trout. Sport with sea-trout can start in April but then fades away until July, when the summer runs come into the river.

## Access

Lovat Estates own most of the Beauly system, and inquiries about their beats and the association water should be made to Lovat Estate Office in Beauly (*telephone* 0463 782205).

Those who are thinking in terms of the upper rivers should contact the Glen Affric Hotel at Cannich (*telephone* 045 65 214), which leases as many beats as it can on the upper rivers, as well as having some magnificent loch fishing for trout.

# 12  The Ness System

The Ness system comprises the rivers and lochs of the north-eastern end of the Great Glen. The Garry is the southernmost river of the system; beyond the watershed lies the Lochy system, flowing south-west to the sea at Fort William.

In draining the mountain ranges to either side of the Great Glen, the Ness system is the largest catchment area in the Highlands. Hourly rates of flow can be quite phenomenal, with more than half eventually flowing down the River Ness through Inverness and out into the Moray Firth.

Due to our need for electrical energy, the Hydro Board has considered the potential of virtually all Highland river systems for power generation, and the Ness system was not found wanting in this respect. Both the rivers Moriston and Garry have been developed in this respect, and it has to be said that the fishing is not what it was. Even so, and despite comparisons with the past, they are still capable of showing an adequate supply of salmon each season – and it does tend to be salmon in these secondary rivers. For some reason, while the sea-trout in the River Ness and Loch Ness can be very good, they do not penetrate much farther into the system.

## RIVER NESS

### Season

15 January to 15 October (best spring and summer).

### Fish and Fishing

There can be little doubt that batches of salmon run the Ness virtually throughout the year on the 5-mile journey from the Moray Firth up to Loch Ness. However, the peaks of activity, and thus of sport, run from the start of the season in January through to the end of May, and then again from late July through to season's end on 15 October.

In recent times early-season fishing tends to have fallen away. No longer can the river produce 100 salmon for the start of the

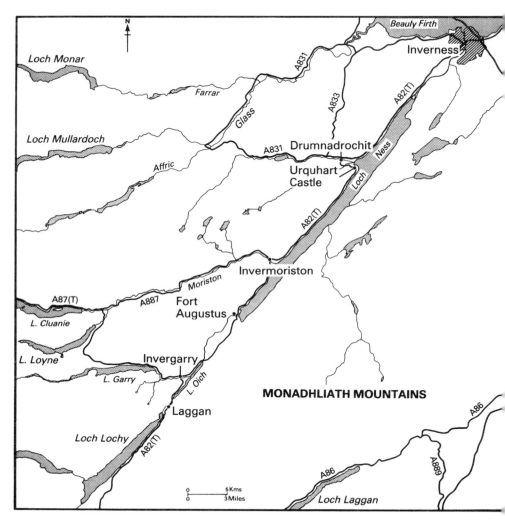

Map 32    *The Ness System*

season. What has been lost on these early spring runs has, however, more than been made up in terms of the greater numbers of summer salmon and grilse. To give some idea of the relative proportions of the summer run compared with the spring run, the Town Water at Inverness, fished by the Inverness Angling Club, in the season of 1988 had only 16 salmon up to June but 523 from June to the end of the season, a ratio of about 1:50.

Much of the early-season fishing on the Ness is with a spinning rod. The Toby spoon is as well favoured here as anywhere, and is particularly useful for swimming across a powerful push of water. Many anglers feel, however, that while they may be great attractors, they do not hook a fish nearly so well as a Devon minnow. The Ness is a big river, and most early-season spinners would choose a 10-foot rod matched with a multiplier or fixed-spool reel, according to taste.

Any early-season fly fishing that is done is with sinking lines and 2- or 3-inch tube flies in patterns such as Yellow and Orange, Willie Gunn, Black and Yellow, and so on. But fly fishing does not really play a great part on the Ness scene until the start of summer sport from June onwards. Then the floating line becomes the number one choice. Flies of size 6 down to 12 are the thing, depending upon water height and temperature, but some of the older generation of Ness fishermen will tell you that a sparsely dressed size 4 has proved its worth time and again on the wide waters of the Ness. The most popular patterns for the Ness include the Stoat's Tail and its silver relation, the Munro Killer, Jeannie and the Shrimp Fly.

Regardless of what size and pattern of fly is chosen, there remains the little matter of casting and presentation. The Ness is a big, wide river. It has to be to carry all the water coming off the enormous catchment area. And therefore, on many occasions, sheer casting range and the ability to fish a long line effectively can be a bonus. Carbon rods of 15 feet are the norm, and 16- and 17-footers not uncommon. Personally, if you have the strength to handle it, I think that there is a great deal to be said for a long rod. My own 17-footer rolls and Spey-casts almost in slow motion, but it throws a long line admirably. But make no mistake – you will be ready for a dram and a long soak in a hot bath after using such a weapon through a long fishing day!

Good numbers of sea-trout run the Ness and on into the loch. They usually start to appear at some time in May, and will then keep coming right through to the end of the season. The season of 1988 produced 426 sea-trout off the Town Water. A rod of 10 or 11 feet, a floating line and a brace of wet flies of about size 8 will take sea-trout on virtually any Scottish sea-trout river. Popular patterns

*Covering the tail of a pool can often be rewarding*

include the Peter Ross, the Teal, Blue and Silver, the Silver Invicta
and Kenny's Killer for the point, and flies such as the Black Pennell,
the Dark Mackerel, Wickham's Fancy and so on for the bob or top
dropper position. My own feeling about flies is that you should be
prepared to go and buy some from the local tackle shop and, at the
same time, see if there is any information available as to who is
catching what, where, when and on what.

   Finally, the Ness season closes with a finale of late-running
salmon. These are not coloured fish; in fact they are spanking fresh,
sea-liced salmon which run the river through September and into
October.

## Access

Working upstream from the mouth of the river, and despite its
relatively short length, the Ness accommodates a number of beats,
as well as the Town Water. The Town Water is next to the tide and
above this is the Ness Castle Water, which is virtually private.

Then comes Laggan, a private beat of only about 600 yards in length but with good streamy water and a particularly nice pool, and finally the two beats owned by Dochfour Estate.

A day ticket can be had for the association water at Inverness, but not for a Saturday, although the weekly ticket is for the full six days of the Scottish salmon week (no fishing on Sundays). Contact:

> J. Graham & Co
> Tackle Dealers
> 71 Castle Street
> Inverness
> *Telephone* 0463 33178

# LOCH NESS

## Season

15 January to 15 October.

## Fish and Fishing

The 25-mile-long Loch Ness can yield salmon on the opening day of the season. At any time of year, it can be a rough place to be out in a boat and the best rule that I can offer to a man standing next to his boat in the morning and eyeing the build-up of long waves with white horse tops is: 'If in doubt, don't.' Certainly, until you have got to know the loch reasonably well you are best advised either to not venture too far or, better still, to hire the help of a gillie or the services of a skilled local.

The fly is fished on Loch Ness, and this method takes many sea-trout, but, for salmon-fishing specialists, the troll is the favoured method. At least two spinning rods will be set up. The inshore rod is known as the 'shore' rod and the outer rod as the 'deep'. Sometimes a short but stiff 'poker' rod will fish a third lure directly in the wake of the boat. Obviously, lures and line lengths vary with conditions and personal tastes, but I might start off with a floating Rapala on 25 yards of line on the 'shore', a Kynoch Killer on 15 yards on the 'poker' and a Toby spoon on the 'deep'. Tackle for trolling should be stout, as each year seems to produce at least one 30-pounder. The most popular areas for trying to contact such fish are off the south bank around Foyers, Invermoriston and Fort Augustus.

## Access

In order to get on to the loch, you must obviously first find a boat. Contact:

> Foyers Hotel
> Foyers
> Inverness–shire
> *Telephone* 045 63 216

> Glenmoriston Estate Keeper
> Leveshid
> Glenmoriston
> Inverness–shire
> *Telephone* 0320 51219

# MORISTON

## Season

15 January to 15 October.

## Fish and Fishing

There is only one short stretch of sluggish water on the entire 25-mile course of the Moriston on its descent to Loch Ness off the mountains above Loch Cluanie. The rest of the river is fast-flowing.

The Hydro Board dammed two lochs on the headwaters of the Moriston and another dam was built some 10 miles downstream to create a head of water for Invermoriston power station. The power station itself is just 300 yards above the outflow of the Moriston into Loch Ness.

The fishing today is very largely confined to a section above Dundreggan and on the lowest section of the river, which provides the best of the Moriston sport. Fish are held here until 1 May, when the compensation flow regime is altered and fish are able to ascend freely up the river. This lower section, which is owned by the Glenmoriston Estate, tends to be rather sluggish and is, indeed, often referred to as the Moriston 'estuary'. For this reason spinning is undoubtedly the preferred method for fishing the opening months of the season. It is fly only on the upper river.

## Access

Glenmoriston Estates has changed hands recently but, at the time of writing, the initial arrangements are that permits are to be handled by:

The Keeper
Levishid
Glenmoriston
*Telephone* 0320 51219

The estate also has boats, outboards and gillies on Loch Ness (see above).

## OICH

### Season

15 January to 15 October.

The River Oich provides the 6-mile connection between Loch Ness and Loch Oich. Besides an early spring run, there are summer runs

*After the springers: early season flyfishing on the River Avon*

of salmon and grilse into its fine pools. The river is divided into three beats, which are privately owned, but days are sometimes available. Tackle and techniques are similar to the Ness except that, because the Oich is on a smaller scale, there is not the same need for long rods and extreme casting range.

## Access

Glen Doe water has three rods per day. Contact:

> Alex MacDonald
> Craig Phadric
> Fort Augustus
> *Telephone* 0397 2566

The Aberchalder Estate stretch can be rented by application to:

> Miss Jean Ellice
> Aberchalder Estate
> Invergarry
> *Telephone* 080 93 3783

> Mr Wernham
> *Telephone* 080 93 201

> Post Office
> Invergarry
> *Telephone* 080 93 201

## GARRY AND LOCH OICH

The Garry is hardly the river that it once was before the days of hydroelectricity, but it can still offer excellent salmon fishing. The fishing on Loch Oich, into which the Garry flows, is let along with the river fishing. The river is fly-only, except on the very short distance from Loch Oich up to the generating station. The loch is fished mainly by the troll, and it is interesting that Loch Oich has, on occasions, produced the first salmon off the entire Ness system.

The fishing on the Garry is 3½ miles, both banks, with 24 named pools being fished by 6 rods. The fishing on Loch Oich, which is included, offers a gillie and two boats with outboards.

## Season

15 January to 15 October.

**Access**

Contact:

R.B. Scott
Post Office
Invergarry
*Telephone* 080 93 201

# 13 Nairn, Moray and Banff

## NAIRN

The source of the Nairn is close to the village of Aberchalder, high in the mountains to the south of Loch Ness. Motorists may wonder about its identity as they cross high above it on the A9 travelling from Perth to Inverness. It is a narrow river, considering its 36-mile length and, perhaps for this reason, readily floods over the flat lands of its lower reaches.

The river in its very uppermost reaches has a tendency towards heavy silting. Moving downstream, however, the river soon enters deep, excellent holding pools, well shaded by bankside vegetation, though these bushes and trees may not please fishermen who are limited in their casting repertoire. The last part of its journey is through flat, rich arable ground on the coastal plain.

### Season

11 February to 30 September (best August–September for salmon, June for sea-trout).

### Fish and Fishing

This is a productive salmon river, if approached at the right time of the season. Spring runs have faded, as everywhere, but salmon are still to be caught in March and April, and sometimes earlier. Sea-trout sport can be excellent in May and June. July can be good for salmon, but the best fishing is normally seen in August and September.

Sea-trout fishing can be very good, and flies such as the Teal, Blue and Silver, the Peter Ross, the Black Pennell and the Mallard and Claret are local favourites. For salmon, some fishermen continue to fish the old favourites such as Thunder and Lightning and Blue Charm, but modernists prefer the hair-winged appeal of flies like the Thunder Stoat, Munro Killer, Hairy Mary, and so on. A rod of 10 feet will serve for sea-trout, and you may choose to fish single-handed for salmon as this is not a wide river. Otherwise, a double-handed carbon rod of 13 or 14 feet will serve admirably.

## Access

Nairn Angling Club has the lower 10 miles of the river, from the estuary to Cantray Bridge, and very good it is too. Contact:

Pat Fraser
The High Street
Nairn
*Telephone* 0667 53038

A section of the river above Cantray Bridge is handled by a hotel who supply permits. Contact:

Clava Lodge Hotel
Culloden Moor
Inverness
*Telephone* 0463 790228

Another hotel handles fishing on the Upper Nairn. For this contact:

Whitebridge Hotel
Stratherick
Gorthleck
*Telephone* 04563 226

## FINDHORN

The Findhorn, one of Scotland's most attractive rivers, has its source high in the Monadhliath Mountains, about 65 miles from the sea. Those miles contain a succession of delightful, fast-flowing streams, runs and pools. Down as far as Dulsie Bridge the river is very open with stretches of open flat land on either bank, except for an occasional conifer plantation. Drainage systems for farming and forestry can create fast floods and, besides the damage to the spawing and nursery areas, believe me, it is no joke when you find the river rising by 2 feet in less than ten minutes.

Below Dulsie Bridge, the river experiences a metamorphosis. The river cascades into a gorge whose sheer sides can be 200 feet high in places. This gorge extends downstream for 20 miles. It makes for rugged scenery and fishing conditions but, if you are fishing it and there has been recent rain on the headwaters, watch out for those fast-rising spates. A rise can also be caused by snow melt in the mountains.

## Season

11 February to 30 September (best February–March for the lower river, August–September for the middle and upper).

## Fish and Fishing

In the opening months of the season, salmon will nose their way up from the estuary and into the gorge. Snow melt helps to keep the temperature of the water low, and fish will ascend no farther until the temperature rises. Some fish may move in April, but it is normally May before any significant runs of fish can be expected to pass beyond the gorge. It is a feature of Findhorn salmon that once they have started to run they move on quickly, and may be up as far as Tomatin within three days.

The early-season fish which are halted in the gorge – the salmon of February and March – may run on the big side. By that I mean that there will be a few 30-pounders as well as plenty of 15–20-pounders.

Grilse start to run towards the end of June, and they will be taken over the entire length of the river. September is the best month on the upper river, as shown in the records for the Drynachan beats of the Cawdor Estates.

RIVER FINDHORN – 3 DRYNACHAN BEATS

Five Year Average Catch

|  | 1988 | 1987 | 1986 | 1985 | 1984 | Total | Average |
|---|---|---|---|---|---|---|---|
| May | 9 | 9 | 17 | 25 | 16 | 76 | 15 |
| June | 4 | 12 | 30 | 26 | 7 | 79 | 16 |
| July | 21 | 4 | 3 | 22 | — | 50 | 10 |
| August | 57 | 6 | 31 | 23 | — | 117 | 23 |
| September | 144 | 93 | 63 | 75 | 27 | 402 | 80 |
| October | 2 | — | — | — | — | 2 | — |
| Totals | 237 | 124 | 144 | 171 | 50 | 726 | 145 |

## Access

Demand for fishing on the Findhorn far exceeds supply. Therefore I have no intention of discussing the maze of beats that are let either on the long term or to individuals who would not give up their

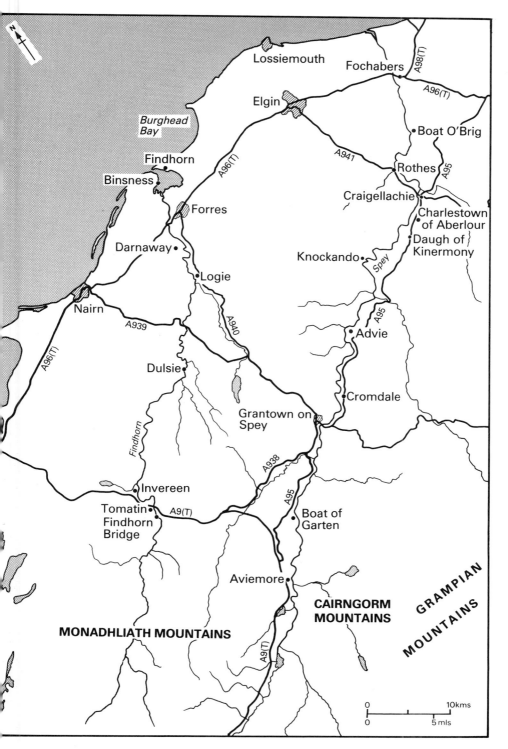

Map 33    *Rivers Findhorn and Spey*

weeks while there is still breath in their bodies. Let me, instead, suggest three possibilities.

There is a stretch of association fishing down at the mouth of the river which is open to visitors, provided that they are staying in the Forres area. Contact:

J. Geddes
Sports Shop
Tolbooth Street
Forres

For the Drynachan beats on the upper river, contact:

The Factor
Cawdor Estate Office
Cawdor
Nairn
*Telephone* 06677 666

Finally, a hotel that may be able to arrange fishing on the upper river:

The Freeburn Hotel
Tomatin
*Telephone* 08082 205

## LOSSIE

The source of the Lossie is the Seven Sisters Spring near Glen Trevie and the river flows for some 35 miles to enter the Moray Firth, sandwiched between the Findhorn and the Spey. With two such outstanding salmon rivers for neighbours, it is perhaps understandable that little is heard of the Lossie, for it is a smaller river which produces fewer fish. Nevertheless, about 150 salmon and hundreds of sea-trout are taken from the Lossie each season.

### Season

11 February to 11 October.

### Fishing

The salmon fishing is at its best late on in the season, during September and October. The smaller sizes of Waddington shanks, armed with a small treble hook, are very popular in all the standard

*Covering the water is the challenge on big rivers like the Spey, Tay and Dee*

patterns, but worm is used heavily in high water. The sea-trout of June, July and August may fall for the charms of any of the standard patterns – Peter Ross, Teal, Blue and Silver, Dunkeld, Black Pennell, Invicta, and so on.

The Lossie flows for its main part through arable land which gives it a gravelly or muddy rather than a rocky bed. Pools tend to be small but deep and there is considerable tree and scrub cover on many stretches.

## Access

Virtually the entire lower river, is fished by the Elgin and District Angling Association. Permits from the following:

Homecrafts
Queens Street
Lossiemouth
*Telephone* 034381 3119

The Angling Centre
Moss Street
Elgin
*Telephone* 0343 7615

The Tackle Shop
118 High Street
Elgin
*Telephone* 0343 3219

The Kellas Estate has the stretch above the Elgin Association water, and day tickets are available:

Kellas Estate
Elgin
*Telephone* 0343 89 343

## SPEY

The Spey is perhaps the most famous salmon river in Britain, perhaps in the world. The upper section can virtually be ignored in terms of salmon fishing, but from Grantown down to the sea there is a fall of some 600 feet in just over 40 miles, creating a fast, turbulent stream that rolls through majestic pools and shallow runs and streams with, in places, the force of a runaway train.

For many fishermen, the Spey represents the ultimate fly-fishing challenge so far as salmon are concerned. No other river is able to test so fully the fisherman's ability to throw a long line and wade deep. In my view, for what it is worth, the Spey should not be seen as a river for the inexperienced, elderly or infirm – certainly not if the most is to be made of it. But for the experienced and capable salmon fisherman – well, there is nowhere quite like it. And it is perhaps the finest sea-trout river in Britain. Who could ask for more?

The Spey is second only to the Tay in terms of catchment area. Four mountain ranges provide a reservoir of snow melt to maintain the river at excellent fishing heights through the spring and into early summer. There are neither natural nor man-made obstructions to bar the passage of fish.

The Spey is different in that it experiences slow, sluggish water only in its upper reaches. That is why, so far as salmon fishing is concerned, the stretches above Grantown can virtually be ignored. I am not saying that salmon will not be caught up at Aviemore and beyond. Far from it. But there really is no comparison between this upper water and the magnificent lower stretches and beats. It is on the lower river that we find the famed names of truly great salmon beats – Castle Grant, Tulchan, Ballindalloch, Pitchroy, Knockando, Laggan, Carron, Wester Elchies, Aberlour, Easter Elchies, Arndilly, Rothes, Aikenway, Delfur, Orton, and Gordon Castle.

## Season

11 February to 30 September (best April–June traditionally for salmon, June–July for sea-trout).

## Fish and Fishing

Traditionally, the Spey showed its best sport with salmon in the opening months of the season. April, May and June are still considered as prime months. But, as on so many if not all rivers, recent times have seen a definite swing towards ever-increasing numbers of summer salmon and grilse. With netting now curtailed, this swing is likely to become even more pronounced.

With regard to sea-trout, the Spey has emerged in recent seasons as perhaps the best river for this species in Britain. The growth rate of Spey sea-trout seems to be excellent. I have seen a bag of seven Spey sea-trout, taken between dusk and midnight on a Saturday night, which weighed a total of more than 30 lb. And the Spey populations contain definite generations of fish with multi-return specimens – a significant proportion surviving spawning, falling back to the sea, and returning in following years.

It is interesting that while most salmon come from the middle and lower river, it is the upper-middle Spey and its tributaries Feshie and Avon which are most noted for sea-trout. Some say that this is only because the lower beats concentrate hard on salmon and grilse through the day and, because the flesh is weak and men must sleep, the sea-trout tend to pass unmolested!

## Tackle and Techniques

There is a great tradition of deep wading, long rods and Spey casting on this river. They combine to allow the fisherman to fish as long a line as possible and to gain what has been described as 'effective water command'. A long line allows you to cover as much water as possible and thus more salmon and, with them, any potential takers. Make no mistake, the man who is capable of throwing the longest length of line and fishing it effectively will, on a river like the Spey, always catch more fish than his less accomplished companions. Of course it is not necessary to throw the full length of a 30-yard line in all Spey pools to be in with a chance, and the 20- and 25-yard casters take their share of fish, but let me just say that the Spey is a river that reminds me of those notes that appeared with monotonous regularity on my reports from school – 'must try harder if he is to achieve any notable success'.

The ability to perform the single and double Spey casts is something that I would advise any salmon fisherman to achieve, but particularly if he intends to fish a river the size of the Spey. Then, in terms of sheer casting range and line control, he will be well advised to use as long a rod as he can comfortably handle. A rod of 15 feet is now widely regarded as the standard general-purpose weapon for salmon fly fishing. But, if you can handle the extra leverage, a rod of 16 or 17 feet gets the job done that little bit more effectively Those who can use the longest lengths of carbon rods are in the minority and personally, while rods up to as much as 20 feet are available, I see my own top limit as a 17-footer, and that is with plenty of log chopping in winter and regular practice through the fishing season.

As to the choice of line, it has to be said that many Spey regulars fish a floating line right through the salmon season. In cold-water conditions, they simply tie on a heavy brass tube fly to attain some depth. This can work well on the Spey because, I would suggest, it is not a deep river. A long line fishes across slowly, giving the big, heavy fly time to sink and fish down to fish lying in perhaps 4 or 5 feet of water. Personally, I feel a lighter fly on a sinking line fishes that little bit more attractively – perhaps a copper or aluminium tube on an intermediate line if the water is fairly low – but there is no denying that local experts take plenty of cold-water salmon on their floating lines and heavy flies.

Some time in May the water temperature will have risen above the threshold of 50°F and then there is no doubt that the floating line is all that is required.

From now on fly sizes vary according to the water temperature. The higher the temperature climbs and the lower the water falls, so the smaller the size of fly that is fished, with sizes ranging from 4 down to 12 in low, warm, summer conditions. Despite all the talk of long rods, once the water levels have fallen many Spey fishermen turn to a single-handed rod of about 10 feet for their summer salmon and grilse fishing and there is no denying that the taking of fish on such sensitive tackle is great fun, if not, perhaps, the most effective method.

The single-handed rod will also serve for sea-trout fishing. Some choose from standard sea-trout flies such as the Peter Ross, the

*One on the bank: the Avon, a tributary of the Spey*

Teal, Blue and Silver, and so on, though personally I tend to fish a Black Pennell on the dropper and a tiny Silver Stoat tube armed with a treble on the point. With such a cast the options are well covered, and you can never be really sure whether your next cast will produce a take from a sea-trout, a grilse or a summer salmon.

Among salmon flies the local favourites include the native Munro Killer, Stewart's Killer, Jeannie, Stoat's Tail, Black Maria, and so on. The Munro Killer may take as many Spey salmon as all the rest put together, because it is so widely used as well as being so attractive to fish. For what it is worth I fish the Munro Killer a lot but, if anything, owe greater allegiance to the Arndilly Fancy, though I insist on tying it fairly sparse, and with a wing at least twice the length of the body dressing. In smaller flies for summer use I have great faith in what has come to be called a Tosh, which is little more than a Stoat's Tail with a yellow hackle. Perhaps I am doing little more than sticking with the advice I gained from an old Spey gillie many seasons ago: 'A fly with black and yellow in its make-up does well here.'

**Access**

Spey fishing is in intense demand and yet, surprisingly, it can be found. Besides the excellent stretches of association water, there are a number of outstanding beats where fishing may be available. On others the fishing is so closely guarded that it may be virtually impossible to discover the identity of the letting agents, let alone contact them. Indeed, many of the beats that I am about to describe give no grounds for much hope but they are, nevertheless, worth approaching with serious inquiries – and an open cheque book. The fisheries below are given in an upstream direction.

*Fochabers*
Contact the Orton Management Company for details of private fishing that may be available.

> Orton Management Co Ltd
> Orton
> Fochabers
> *Telephone* 034388 240

*Craigellachie*
Advance booking is not available but you might take a chance on gaining access through:

> W. Roy
> Craigmichael
> Maggieknockater
> *Telephone* 03404 387

*Aberlour*
Some tickets may be available on the town water, but only to visitors staying in the village. Talk to Mr Mitchell at Munro's Tackle Shop (*telephone* 03405 428). Alternatively, try the Dowans Hotel (*telephone* 03405 488), who may be able to arrange private fishing for their guests.

*Ballindalloch Castle*
Private fishing with gillies on two Spey beats and on the very productive Avon tributary. Contact:

> Mr Russell
> The Estate Office
> Ballindalloch Castle
> Banffshire
> *Telephone* 08072 205

*Tulchan*
Tulchan Estate has four outstanding beats with gillies. Occasional rods may be available for non-residents, or you can choose to stay with them at Tulchan Lodge, whose guests receive priority. Contact:

> The Factor
> Tulchan Estate Office
> Advie
> near Grantown-on-Spey
> *Telephone* 080 75 200

*Castle Grant*
Upstream from Tulchan are the three outstanding beats on Castle Grant, all let with a resident gillie. Contact:

> Hugh Blakeney
> Seafield Estate Office
> Grantown-on-Spey
> *Telephone* 0479 2529

*Grantown*
Strathspey Angling Association offers weekly permits on 7 miles of the Spey and 12 miles of the tributary River Dulnain. Visitors must reside in the specified local area. Hundreds of salmon and over 1,000 sea-trout are expected in a normal season. Contact:

> Mortimer's Tackle
> The High Street
> Grantown-on-Spey
> *Telephone* 0479 2684

*Boat of Garten*
This is about as high as you would want to travel up the Spey so far as salmon are concerned. The river does not have the same flow now as on lower stretches, and there are deeper pools. Abernethy Angling Association makes permits available to visitors staying in the local area. Tickets from:

> Ban o' Gar Stores
> Boat of Garten
> *Telephone* 0479 83 372

## DEVERON

The Deveron rises in the hills to the north of Strathdon, in west Aberdeenshire. After being joined by the Black Water tributary it flows north-east down Strathglass to the town of Huntly, a principal fishing centre, where it is joined by another major tributary, the River Bogie. From Huntly the river flows for 22 miles through mainly arable lands to Turriff, picking up the Isla tributary on the way. From Turriff to Banff on the coast is a flow of some 11 miles of long, deep pools and gravelly runs and streams.

## Season

11 February to 31 October (best September–October for salmon, July–August for grilse, June–July for sea-trout).

## Fish and Fishing

The Deveron has a fine reputation for both salmon and sea-trout fishing. It is very much a spate river, however, so it needs rain and spates to show its best, after which the sport can be tremendous. In most seasons more than 1,500 salmon are taken, and an even greater number of sea-trout. And, besides sheer quantities, the Deveron is noted for the quality and size of its fish. A salmon of 61 lb was taken by Mrs Morrison in 1924 and, while it was not big enough to beat Miss Ballantine's record Tay fish, it is reputed to be the biggest British salmon taken on a fly. The Deveron also has a reputation as a producer of giant sea-trout, with an 18-pounder taken in the late 1960s being a notable example in modern times. As one Deveron man put it to me, they reckon that a 'good' sea-trout is one of 12–13 lb, but an 8–10-pounder would be nothing much to boast about.

When spinning in the opening and closing months of the season, Deveron fishermen tend to stick with the Devon minnow in black

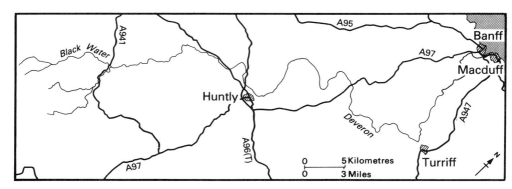

Map 34   *The Deveron*

and gold, brown and gold or yellow and green (Yellow Belly), or a Toby spoon.

For fly fishing, Deveron salmon seldom if ever require the big sizes of fly that we associate with other rivers. A rod of about 15 feet forms the basis of the outfit. Flies of sizes 4 or 6 will be used in spring, reducing to an 8 in May and down to 10 and 12 in summer. Popular patterns include the Jeannie, Munro's Killer and Ally's Shrimp. Sea-trout are taken on the standard patterns and something called the 'Hydroelectric Blue' – which, I am told, has 'some red and pale blue, a bit of teal and a pinch of tippet . . .' I will have to get one of these flies for dissection next time I am up Deveron way!

## Access

It can be said that much of the River Deveron is available to visitors, and it is true that local estates and hotels offer some excellent fishing. It is equally true that anybody who fishes the Deveron will recognize the value of what he has and ensure that he makes his repeat booking in plenty of time for the following season. However, here are some suggestions.

A number of beats on the middle river are handled by G. Mason, Sports Shop, Gordon Street, Huntly (*telephone* 0466 2482). Also try Jay Tee Sports Shop, Low Street, Banff (*telephone* 02612 5821), and I. Masson, 14 Main Street, Turriff (*telephone* 0888 62428) for the Turriff Angling Association stretch.

A number of hotels can arrange fishing on the Deveron. Contact:

County Hotel
High Street
Banff
*Telephone* 02612 5353

Forbes Arms Hotel
Rothiemay
*Telephone* 046681 248

The Belldorney Castle Water is handled by Bell Ingram, Estate Agents, 7 Walker Street, Edinburgh.

# 14　Aberdeenshire

## YTHAN

The Ythan (pronounced eye-than) has its novel source in a spring-fed well in the schoolmaster's garden at the eastern end of Strathbogie, known as the Wells of Ythan. From the source it is just over 30 miles as the river flows through lush agricultural land to the Ythan estuary at Newburgh, some 4 miles from Ellon and 14 miles to the north of Aberdeen.

### Season

11 February to 31 October (best August–September for salmon, June–October for sea-trout).

### Fish and Fishing

The Ythan is a widely known and very important sea-trout fishery, with the best of the fishing being enjoyed in the estuary. Also, the river has been producing steadily increasing numbers of salmon towards the close of the season.

The estuary is known as the Newburgh Fishings, and is owned by the Udny and Dudwick Estate. The water is fished both from the banks and from boats, depending on the state of the tide. Bank fishing is at its best after the top of the tide if just beyond the turn of the tide after low water. Boat fishing then begins halfway up the incoming tide. There are 17 recognized pools on the stretch and fishing is by fly or spinner. It can be said that the fly is the most popular method, but it will often be presented on a spinning rod. Because of the need to cast a fairly long line and the frequent presence of weed that may need removing from the hook – much easier with spinning tackle, which can be simply wound in – standard Ythan tackle is a spinning rod and fixed-spool reel, but with a spiral lead and swivel on the trace to which a tube fly is attached. I have some of these Ythan tubes on my desk as I write, a memento of a recent visit, and they are simple but very effective designs typified by a bright tinsel body and trailing wings of brown, badger or white whole hackle feathers. In the water they look for all the world like the small sandeels which are present in the estuary in good numbers.

At other states of the tide, and particularly in the vicinity of the road bridge, smaller flies, presented on proper fly rods, reels and lines, can be very effective. Popular patterns include the Peter Ross, the Teal, Blue and Silver, the Dunkeld, the Grey Monkey, and so on. Smaller flies are used as the tide ebbs, from a 10 right down to a 12 or 14 when the tide is right out.

The eastern shore of the estuary is part of the Forvie Nature Reserve and there are some restrictions on access. I found the presence of great rafts of preening eider duck to be a charming part and parcel of the Ythan experience.

The catch figures set out below are said to show a minimum for the number of fish taken in recent seasons. Up till now, although the situation has recently changed, the water was let on a day–ticket basis, and it has been notoriously difficult to obtain accurate catch figures. The fishery manager, Eddie Forbes, assured me that in his opinion, based on twenty-six years' experience in his post, the true figures might be as much as twice those shown. The records certainly make it clear why the Ythan estuary has gained the reputation of being the finest sea-trout stretch in Europe.

CATCHES FROM THE NEWBURGH FISHING, YTHAN ESTUARY

Sea Trout

| | 1979 | 1980 | 1981 | 1982 | 1983 | 1984 | 1985 | 1986 | 1987 | 1988 | 3 Yr Avrge | 10 Yr Avrge |
|---|---|---|---|---|---|---|---|---|---|---|---|---|
| Jan | — | — | — | — | — | — | — | — | — | — | — | — |
| Feb | — | — | — | 21 | — | — | — | — | — | — | — | 2 |
| Mar | — | — | — | 12 | — | 1 | — | — | — | — | — | 1 |
| April | — | 4 | — | 36 | 20 | 6 | 32 | 31 | 44 | — | 25 | 20 |
| May | 11 | 44 | 6 | 79 | 100 | 31 | 129 | 281 | 231 | 136 | 216 | 105 |
| June | 421 | 130 | 190 | 275 | 207 | 184 | 193 | 237 | 438 | 235 | 300 | 251 |
| July | 418 | 209 | 368 | 441 | 315 | 274 | 328 | 361 | 506 | 337 | 401 | 356 |
| Aug | 693 | 344 | 631 | 615 | 565 | 329 | 554 | 590 | 552 | 495 | 546 | 531 |
| Sept | 260 | 207 | 510 | 774 | 334 | 227 | 295 | 496 | 503 | 357 | 452 | 396 |
| Oct | 11 | 3 | 10 | 14 | 43 | 3 | 26 | 91 | 16 | 64 | 57 | 25 |
| Total | 1,814 | 941 | 1,715 | 2,267 | 1,584 | 1,055 | 1,557 | 2,087 | 2,290 | 1,624 | 2,000 | 1,687 |

Average weight: 2 lb

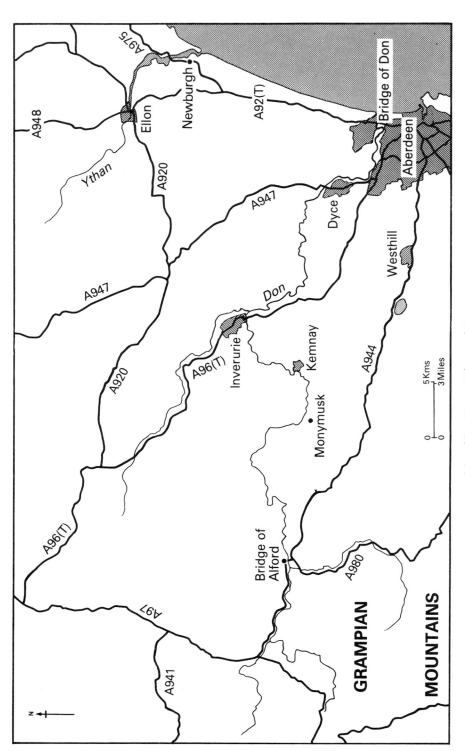

Map 35   *Rivers Ythan and Don*

Salmon and Grilse

| | 1979 | 1980 | 1981 | 1982 | 1983 | 1984 | 1985 | 1986 | 1987 | 1988 | 3 Yr Avrge | 10 Yr Avrge |
|---|---|---|---|---|---|---|---|---|---|---|---|---|
| Jan | — | — | — | — | — | — | — | — | — | — | — | — |
| Feb | — | — | — | — | — | — | — | — | — | — | — | — |
| Mar | — | — | — | — | — | — | — | — | — | — | — | — |
| April | — | — | — | — | — | — | — | — | — | — | — | — |
| May | — | — | — | 1 | — | — | — | — | — | — | — | 0.1 |
| June | — | 1 | — | — | — | — | — | — | — | — | — | 0.1 |
| July | 1 | 1 | 1 | — | 2 | 1 | 3 | 2 | 1 | — | 1 | 1.2 |
| Aug | 1 | 12 | 15 | 41 | 22 | 10 | 3 | 14 | 4 | 2 | 7 | 12.4 |
| Sept | 22 | 27 | 64 | 91 | 58 | 26 | 3 | 69 | 43 | 13 | 41.6 | 40.3 |
| Oct | 1 | 6 | — | — | 8 | 2 | — | 22 | 1 | — | 7.6 | 4.0 |
| Total | 25 | 47 | 80 | 133 | 90 | 39 | 9 | 107 | 49 | 15 | 57.2 | 59.4 |

Average weight: 10½ lb

## Access

Up until recent times the Newburgh fishing was let on a day-ticket basis, but in 1989 it was announced that there was to be 'an opportunity to purchase a 21-year lease for a specified week for up to 4 rods' on 3 miles with 3 beats being fished in rotation. The lease can be sold, assigned or sublet, subject to certain terms. Accommodation is offered as a package with one of the beats. Two boats are provided with each of the Middle and Lower Beats, and so on and so forth. To my mind, it is a very interesting offer and a very worthy alternative to timeshares in perpetuity for those with between £2,500 to £10,000 per rod per week to spend.

A stretch of river which includes the Mill Pool has been kept out of the lease scheme and reserved for use by the local angling club, which, so far as I have been able to ascertain, has not yet decided whether it will be offering visitors' tickets.

Do not think that this all implies a closed shop on the Ythan estuary for the next 21 years. It may be that some of the weeks will not be taken, or not fully booked, so lets may be available.

For full details of the Lease Scheme contact:

Jonathan Kennedy
Humberts
25 Grosvenor Street
London W1X 9FE
Telephone 01 629 6700

For other details contact:

> Eddie Forbes
> Fishery Manager
> 3 Lea Cottages
> Newburgh
> *Telephone* 035 86 297

## Other Fishing

While Newburgh is undoubtedly the cream of the Ythan fishing, there is more access to be had on upstream stretches. Just above the estuary permission to fish 3 miles, both banks, may be had from the Auchamacoy Estate Office (*telephone* 0358 20291).

Farther upstream, in the area of Methlick, the Haddo Estate single-bank fishing is operated by the Haddo House Angling Club. Some day tickets may be available from James French, Main Street, Methlick, who is also able to arrange some fishing on another single-bank stretch. *Telephone* 065 12 213.

*Big river tactics – fishing out the cast on the middle Dee*

# DON

The Don rises in wild remote country in the Grampian Mountains. The first half of the river's course is steep and fast through wooded hills. A number of tributaries join the river up here. Then, just a few miles below Alford, the gradient fades and the river passes through flatter land leading to water meadows rather in the style of an English south-country river. Indeed, while trout fishing is outside the scope of this book, the Don is generally recognized as offering some of the very finest trout fishing in Scotland. In terms of rivers it has virtually no rivals in this respect. And it is dry-fly country where patterns such as the Greenwell's Kite's Imperial and Blue Quill are cast delicately to ride jauntily over the neb of a feeding brown trout. But I digress, so back to salmon and sea-trout.

The Don's most important tributary is the Urie, which enjoys a high reputation for its sea-trout fishing. Urie and Don join at Inverurie, some 16 miles from Aberdeen.

## Season

11 February to 31 October (best February–April and September–October for salmon, May–August for sea-trout).

## Fish and Fishing

While most about are losing theirs, the Don, like its close neighbour the Dee, is still able to boast something of a spring run of salmon. Most of the action takes place on the lower river at this early stage of the season and, while the fly is fished, and hard, many of the Don's springers fall to the seductive allures of a Devon minnow or a Toby spoon.

It is during the summer and back-end fishing that salmon and grilse can be found virtually throughout the entire length of the river, with the uppermost reaches only really starting to produce salmon in September and October. Poaching and pollution are two problems that have had to be faced on the Don but, particularly now that the estuary nets are no longer in operation, things are looking well for the Don and its salmon.

Sea-trout can provide good sport from May through to August. In high water, spinners such as the Krill, Mepps and Sutherland Special, which can only be described as looking 'like a bent Devon with wings and a diving vane' but which can be highly effective for both migratory species, may be the things but, as the water levels fall, the fly comes into its own, with any of the Scottish traditionals doing well.


**Access**

How on earth am I to set about describing access to the Don? Few people realise that there are, in fact, 63 separate beats on this river. so let me make a start at Aberdeen.

*Grandhome Fishings*

> Marion Webster
> D. Wardhaugh and Son
> Kirriemuir
> *Telephone* 0575 73060

*Upper Parkhill, Upper and Lower Fintray*

> Jas Somers and Son
> 40 Thistle Street
> Aberdeen

Kintore Fishings

> Kintore Arms Hotel
> Kintore
> *Telephone* 0476 32216

*Manar and Inverurie Fishings*

> J. J. Watson
> Ironmonger
> Market Place
> Inverurie
> *Telephone* 0467 20321 and ask for Bert Brand

*Kemnay Fishings (single bank)*

> Mrs Milton
> Kemnay House
> Kemnay
> *Telephone* 0467 42220

*Monymusk Fishings*

> Grant Arms Hotel
> Monymusk
> *Telephone* 04677 226

*Forbes Estates*

> Estate Office
> Whiteford
> by Alford
> *Telephone* 0336 226

*Haughton Fishings*

> Haughton Arms Hotel
> Alford
> *Telephone* 0336 2108

*Kildrummy Fishings*

> Mr T. Hilary
> *Telephone* 033 65 208

*Glenkindie Fishings*

> Glenkindie Arms Hotel
> Glenkindie
> *Telephone* 097 53 288

*Tornashean Fishing*

> Mr McIntosh
> Donview
> Strathdon
> *Telephone* 097 52 302

*Edinglassie and Candacraig Fishings*

> Colquhonnie Hotel
> Strathdon
> *Telephone* 097 52 210

## ABERDEENSHIRE DEE

In many ways the Dee is similar to the Spey. Both have spring and early-summer water levels maintained by snow melt at their sources, both of which are found in the high mountains of the Cairngorms. The Dee, however, differs from the Spey in that it is steepest in its upper section, then has a steadily shallower gradient, softening in its middle section and finally flowing through gentle arable country on its final stage of the journey to the sea at Aberdeen.

The Dee is a comparatively long river, measuring approximately

90 miles from the sea to its principal sources on Ben Macdhui and Braeriach, both at a height of about 4,000 feet.

The most important part of the Dee for fishing, where the great salmon beats are found, is the lower 60 miles, from Peterculter close to Aberdeen up as far as Cambus O'May. But that statement must be kept in context. Upstream of Cambus O'May you will discover such famous beats as Abergeldie; Balmoral and Invercauld – so it is all relative.

From Ballater, just upstream of the Cambus O'May beat, the Dee flows swiftly down to Aboyne to create excellent fishing on beats such as Glen Tanar and Birse Castle. From Aboyne to Banchory the Dee maintains its exceptional standards on beats which are virtually everyday names in the world of salmon fishing – Dess, Carlogie, Ballogie, Woodend, Cairnton, Inchmarlo and Blackhall. It was on Cairnton that the late Arthur Wood perfected his famous greased-line technique. Below Banchory there is still 20 miles of river before it enters Aberdeen on the coast, including superb beats such as Crathes, Drum and Park on the left bank and Durris, Tilbourie and Altries on the right. It is a feature of Dee beats that so many of them are single-bank only. Indeed, out of 45 recognized Dee salmon beats 39 have just one side of the river. In its final 7 miles the river does not fall into the category of a great salmon water. Here the river flows through Aberdeen suburbs and parkland in a slow, sluggish fashion, though that is not to say that this final stretch cannot yield fish.

## Season

1 February to 30 September.

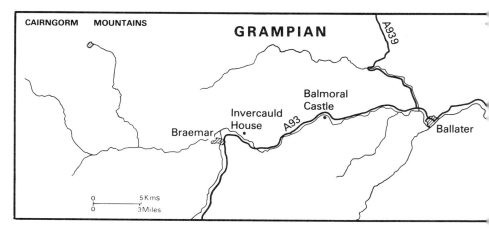

Map 36

*Best times for salmon*
Below Banchory, February–May and September; Banchory to
Cambus O'May, February, April–June and September; above
Cambus O'May, April–June and September

*Sea-trout*   June and July.

## Fish and Fishing

There are no artificial or natural obstructions to fish running the
Dee until they reach the Linns, several miles above Braemar. This
is of great significance in terms of the fish and fishing. With
springers given easy access to the headwaters, the tendency seen on
so many hydroized rivers for the spring runs to dwindle and fade,
to be replaced by heavier numbers of summer salmon and grilse, is
avoided. On the Dee, even the Linns are not impassable, given a
suitable height of water, and so, in relative terms, the spring run is
left to prosper and continue. I say 'in relative terms' because there
are other, external, factors that affect the spring runs and, while it
may not have suffered as badly as other Scottish rivers, it is true and
sad to say that the early-season Dee runs are not quite what they
used to be. But, in the modern age and in comparative terms, the
Dee remains an outstanding producer of early-season salmon. In
terms of numbers alone, it is fair to say that the Dee produces
spring salmon fishing that is second to none in Britain. And, what
is most encouraging, there are signs that the Dee may be starting to
produce even more spring fish and, with netting having been
stopped, the lower and middle river may once again return to their
former glory.

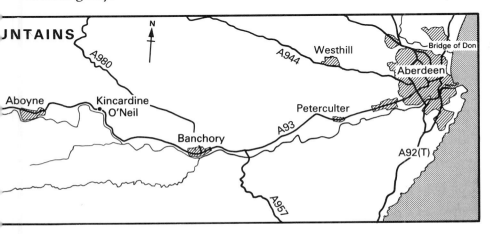

*deenshire Dee*

Runs begin to dwindle somewhat but then pick up again usually towards the end of May with the runs of grilse and summer salmon, with sport picking up again in August and September. Evidence suggests that an autumn run of salmon may be re-establishing itself on the Dee, and older fishermen may remember the time when the Dee fishing continued into October. What this autumn run will produce time alone will tell.

Netting on the mouth of the Dee has stopped since the netting stations were bought by the Atlantic Salmon Conservancy Trust. Some may question what effects this may have on the long-term fishing prospects, the nature of the salmon runs, and so on, but early results are quite outstanding. For example, one middle beat has broken all past records in salmon caught, and the sea-trout catch has actually trebled in the short space of three years. As they say, it is all very encouraging, to say the least.

## Tackle and Techniques

Speaking for myself – and many others, I dare say – I would not think of using any other method than the fly on such a river as the Dee. As one man who has good access to prime beats on the river put it to me: 'Nowadays, I think I would have to apologize to any salmon that I did not catch on the fly.' And yet there is no denying that a great deal of spinning is done on Dee waters in the opening months of the season. Take a 9- or 10-foot rod, attach a multiplier or fixed-spool reel and throw out a Devon minnow of appropriate size and colour, or a Toby or Blair spoon if you must, but it just isn't for me. It is not that I find fly fishing to be more sporting, but it is certainly more challenging, and I find spinning so boring. But, leaving personal feelings out of it, the Dee seldom colours badly, even in spate, and, believe me, I am firmly of the opinion that if those who fish rivers such as the Dee are prepared to go to the bother of learning and practising the roll and Spey casts they will certainly enjoy the eventual satisfaction of being able to beat the spinners both in terms of success and satisfaction, not to mention enjoyment. My apologies to spinners, but at least I have stored up this outpouring of feelings until I reached this fine fly water.

For early-season salmon fishing, Dee fish will move well to the standard Scottish tube flies such as the Willie Gunn (what an outstanding fly!) the Garry, the Black and Yellow, Black and Orange, and so on. Rods in the 15-foot class and a medium sinker, or an intermediate for shallower pools, complete the outfit.

In summer I would tend to stick with the 15-footer but instead of one capable of handling AFTM 11 and 12 lines I would choose a

*Three from the Dee – a fine catch of fresh-run Aberdeenshire fish, each one over 10 lb*

more sensitive alternative to handle AFTM 9 and 10. In the gin-clear waters of the Dee, I feel that a long leader, the length of the rod, has definite advantages. Fairly sparse dressings of flies such as Blue Charm, Hairy Mary, Logie, Stoat, Silver Stoat, Munro Killer and so on will serve well once the water temperature is above 50°F, in sizes 12 down to 8, with an occasional resort to a size 6 in a full river.

As an alternative to the sensitive 15-footer for floating-line use in summer a good case can be made for a rod of about 13 feet, or a single-handed 10- or 11-footer, which many find great fun as well as doubling for sea-trout, which many more people are now taking an interest in.

## Access

Most of the best beats are let on a weekly or fortnightly basis to fishers who have the sense to hold hard onto what they have got. Demand for Dee fishing, certainly at the favourable times of the season, runs miles ahead of the available supply. Some suggestions can be made, however, as to where you might start to make your inquiries.

Just two beats are let on a daily basis. These are the Kincaussie and Ardoe beats near Maryculter. Thankfully, the use of prawn and shrimp has recently been banned. Season tickets are also available. Contact:

Sonja Murdoch
North Lodge
Kincaussie
Maryculter
*Telephone* 0224 732266

Banchory Lodge Hotel leases rods on various beats as well as having its own excellent beat, which includes the junction with the River Feugh tributary. Contact:

Banchory Lodge Hotel
Banchory
Kincardineshire
*Telephone* 03302 2625

High on the upper river is the Mar Lodge water, including the Linns. Contact:

Mar Lodge
Braemar
Aberdeenshire
*Telephone* 033 83 216

For further information on the availability of Dee fishing and accommodation contact: Bro-Dee Fishing Tackle, Aboyne (*telephone* 0339 2272) or write to any of the following letting agents:

James Thorburn
Birkwood
Aboyne
Aberdeenshire

Macsport
Ballater Road
Aboyne
Aberdeenshire

Graham Scott
Granville Lodge
Aboyne
Aberdeenshire

# 15   The East Coast

## BERVIE

The Bervie flows down from the hills past Glenbervie before skirting to the east of the Howe of the Mearns and on to the sea at Inverbervie. Perhaps its most interesting geographical feature is that as a result of wind and tide action a gravel bar can form across the river mouth and thus bar the passage of migratory fish. When this happens, the bar is simply dug away mechanically.

It is perhaps best regarded as a sea-trout rather than a salmon fishery, though very large salmon have been taken off it, including a 50-pounder back in the 1930s – a tremendous size considering the nature of this small river.

Tackle suitable for the North Esk (see below) will also serve admirably on the Bervie.

The sea-trout fishing is at its best in June and July. Salmon start one month later, and steadily build up to a peak in October.

### Season

16 February to 31 October.

### Access

As on the North Esk, some of the fishing is let to rod and line interests by a netting company. For details of the estuary fishing, Contact:

>   Joseph Johnston and Sons Ltd
>   3 America Street
>   Montrose
>   *Telephone* 0674 72666

Upstream, from Arbuthnott up to the A94 road bridge, is fished by the Laurencekirk Angling Club. Fly-only, except in high water, when spinning is allowed. For day and weekly tickets, contact:

>   J. Mowatt
>   111 High Street
>   Laurencekirk
>   *Telephone* 056 17 319

## NORTH ESK

The sources of the North Esk are recognized as two streams tumbling down from the Grampian Mountains. These are the Waters of Mark and Lee. The Lee flows into Loch Lee, which has been dammed and impounded to provide a water supply to Stonehaven and much of South Kincardine. The Mark and Lee join at Invermark to form the North Esk, and the river is soon joined by the Water of Tarf, another important spawning tributary.

From Loch Lee down to the Loups of the Burn (which are a series of falls), a distance of about 15 miles, the river flows down the heather- and rowan-clad Glen Esk. Two notable beats in this stretch are Invermark and Millden. A fish pass was installed on the Loups back in the 1950s to improve the salmon's access to the upper river. But, because of its turbulence and gorge-like nature, the river in the area of the Loups is not easily fished, and most fishers find it is best approached with spinner or bait.

After the North Esk emerges from the gorge it runs on to the sea through fine farmland in a rich series of long holding pools, picking up various tributaries on the way. It is on this lower section that we find beats the like of Gannochy, Arnhall, Dalladies, Stracathro, Inglismaldie, and so on. Note that some pools on the river below Edzell can be fairly treacherous to the wading fisherman, because of the nature of their bedrock. So, if you are unsure, go cautiously, feeling your way with a wading stick, and take extra-special care if fishing late for sea-trout.

### Season

16 February to 31 October (best February–May and September–October for salmon, June–July for sea-trout).

### Fishing

The North Esk is very much a spate river and is prone to low water levels in summer. Perhaps that is one reason why the river is at its best at the opening and close of the season, rather than in summer.

Those who choose to spin the North Esk, when they are allowed, like to use a lightweight Devon minnow, either wooden or plastic, in conjunction with a weight up the trace, such as a spiral lead attached above the swivel some 2 feet above the spinner. The weight gets well down towards the river bed but the minnow, being nearly buoyant, fishes up from it and thus fishes in a very attractive manner while avoiding at least some snags. The Devon

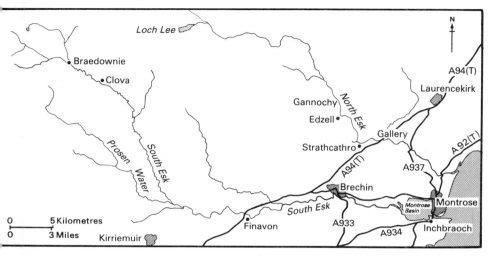

Map 37   *North and South Esk*

will be in the 2–3-inch class for cold-water fishing, and popular colours include the blue-and-silver for early season and the black-and-gold, brown-and-gold, or yellow belly. As an alternative, and a particularly effective one in streamier water, a Toby can be tried in colours such as silver, gold or zebra.

In summer, when spinning for sea-trout on the heels of a spate, small silver and copper Tobys are useful, as is the little Mepps spoon.

Fly fishermen normally choose to fish a 2-inch tube fly in cold-water conditions – a Garry for high water, an Orange and Black or Yellow and Black when the water is clearing, and an all-black Stoat's Tail when it is low and clear – and a Willie Gunn at virtually any time. These flies are for spring. Later in the season, even at its close, such big flies are no longer required – stick to a range of sizes from 4 down to as small as a 12 for low-water summer use.

For sea-trout, on a single-handed rod of about 10 or 11 feet, most who know the North Esk well will probably choose to fish either a small tube fly or a 'wee double' in size 10 or 12, with an equally small dropper. The Stoat and Silver Stoat make up into excellent tube flies.

## Access

At Montrose the netting company has in recent times made two beats and a stretch of fly-only trout and sea-trout fishing available

*Snow and ice is no deterrent to the salmon angler*

to rod and line fishermen. I have been told that the fishing on Canterlands and Gallery beats, which is normally fly-only except in spring and high water, can be excellent. Contact:

Joseph Johnston and Sons Ltd
Salmon Fishers
3 America Street
Montrose
*Telephone* 0674 72666

Burn House has the fishing in the gorge, including the Loups. Worm may be used in a spate; otherwise fly or spinner. A cottage is available. Contact:

The Controller
Burn House
Glenesk
Edzell
*Telephone* 035 64281

Burn Beat is, in fact, two rotating single-bank beats with no restrictions on tackle. Contact:

R. Burnett, Gamekeeper
Sandhill Cottage
Edzell
*Telephone* 035 64 505

Gannochy Estate has three beats, which are fly-only except in spate. Two rods to a beat. The fishing up here does not really start until June. Contact:

R. Ramage
Head Keeper
Gannochy Estate
Edzell
*Telephone* 035 64 7331

Day tickets are sometimes available for the Craigo Beat from Montrose Angling Club. Contact:

G. Luke
3 Meriden Street
Montrose
*Telephone* 0674 73535

## SOUTH ESK

The headwaters of the South Esk are of little interest to the fisherman until the river is swelled by its joining with the White Water close to Braedounie at the head of Glen Clova. The fall in Glen Clova is relatively small, with the river wandering over gravel beds of most significance for spawning purposes. Then, as the river emerges from the foot of Glen Clova, the character of the South Esk is transformed, through attractive holding pools over a rocky course, the river soon being swelled in size by its meeting with the Prosen tributary. Below Justinhaugh the river is not quite so rocky, its bed mainly consisting of gravel, but from here down to the Montrose basin is excellent fishing, particularly for sea-trout.

Early-season salmon fishing is limited in extent by a dyke on the river at Kinnaird, near Brechin, which creates a temperature pool which fish will not pass until the water temperature is up into the forties. Tackle and techniques for those planning a trip to the South Esk are, for all practical purposes, identical to those for the North Esk.

**Season**

16 February to 31 October.

**Access**

The House of Dun beat, upstream of Bridge of Dun, fishes well for sea-trout in the later half of the season – from mid-May through virtually to the end of the season. Salmon and grilse start to arrive in June and, like the sea-trout, continue through the season. Contact:

Mrs J. Philips
Broomlee House
by Montrose
*Telephone* 067 481 202

# 16   Tay and its Tributaries

## TAY

### Season

15 January to 15 October.

### Best Times

The spring run into the Tay, once world-famous in terms of quality and quantity, is but a shadow of its former self. Perhaps the District Salmon Fishery Board's attempts to improve access and runs into the Lochay and Lyon tributaries may see a reversal in the presently declining early-season fortunes. Time alone will tell the outcome. In the meantime, for the purposes of this book, but not without some small measure of reserve, I shall give the best times for the river on rather more of a traditional basis than that which a modern realist might appreciate, and trust that the Tay will soon return to its old self and not leave me embarrassed when I describe January–March as the best time up on Loch Tay though so few fish have been caught in recent opening months. All I can advise, in taking a Tay fishing, is to ask to see up-to-date catch returns, on a monthly basis. So, with these reservations, let me describe the traditional if not necessarily immediately contemporary pattern of best fishing times on the Tay system.

*Loch Tay*   January–March
*Upper Tay*   January–March and, more realistically, September–October
*Middle Tay* January–May and, again more realistically, September–October
*Lower Tay*   We all hope that fishing will improve in the traditional months of January–May but, in modern seasons, August–October is way out in front.

Something else that must be mentioned in regard to 'best times' is the closure, albeit on a temporary basis, of the Scone netting operations, and the increased time of the weekend 'slap', when nets cannot be operated. Equally, everybody is waiting to see what decision will be made in regard to the uppermost nets belonging to the trustees for Viscount Stormont, who currently have an agree-

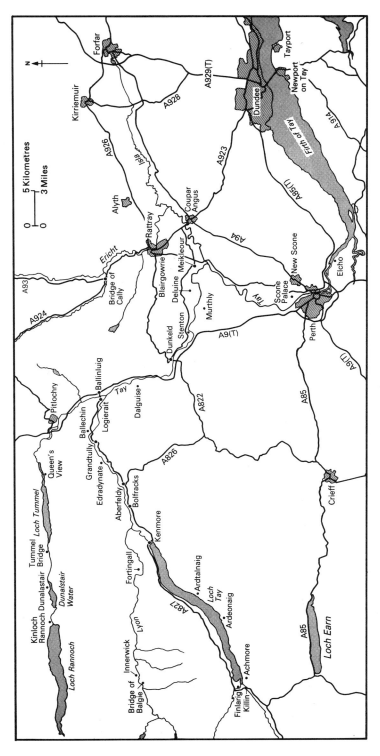

Map 38  *The Tay and its Tributaries*

ment not to net, which will expire in the near future. Certainly the removal of the Scone nets produced an immediate improvement in sea-trout catches and many beats have already seen an improvement in summer and autumn salmon catches, but what proportion of this has been due to the exceptionally wet summer in 1988 and how much to the removal of the nets has not yet been firmly ascertained.

Certainly there is no doubt that less or no netting will inevitably mean more salmon, grilse and sea-trout being taken on rod and line, but the hard thing to determine is how much, where and when.

## Tackle and Technique

The tackle and technique for fishing the Spey have been well documented. Because of its size and scope – it is the biggest salmon river in Scotland – the great majority of fishing, certainly on the middle and lower Tay, is done with the spinning rod. Indeed, to suggest the use of a fly rod on some Tay beats has been described as something of a gillie's joke.

My own preference for big-river spinning is towards something of an extreme in rod length. My principal weapon is a 12-footer which, matched with a multiplier reel, will hurl heavy lures on heavy line for great distances. A great many different lures are used, but personally I tend to limit myself to Devon minnows, usually in brown-and-gold and red-and-gold or similar, and the larger class of Toby spoons. I find the 18-gram has just the right combination of size with a relatively easy weight to produce an attractive swimming action.

The main alternative to spinning is to get afloat out on to the fat Tay pools in a boat. The method is known as harling and involves trailing three lures behind the boat on set lengths of line. The fisherman has little to do, leaving it all to the boatman, until the rod bends and the reel screeches. Some would describe it as the depths of boredom and the least attractive method of salmon fishing, reminiscent of commercial long-lining, but there is no denying its effectiveness. Indeed, this was the method employed by Miss Ballantine's father to hook her record-breaking Tay salmon.

Some of us, however, just cannot resist getting out the fly rod, even if it is just for a few hours break from the monotony of spinning. Some lower beats are virtually unfishable with fly but others offer opportunities, at least for those who are prepared to wade deep and use a long rod and are able to Spey-cast effectively. When I say a long rod I really do mean just that. Some water can be

*Harling: the only way to properly cover the lies on a big river*

covered with a 15-footer, particularly on the upper beats, but let me tell you that one Tay gillie, on seeing my 17-footer, described it as a 'grand wee rod'! He used an 18-footer and was saving up his tips to be able to purchase a 20-footer – 'Noo, that's what I call a fushing rod,' he said seriously.

The fly-fishing opportunities are at their best during the summer and autumn months, and it is wisely said that the Tay fishes best when it is just on the low side. You should not need to go too small, however, and something like a size 4 down to an 8 should prove useful, in patterns such as Munro Killer, Hairy Mary, Shrimp Flies, and so on.

The upper river and tributaries are less dependent upon spinning and harling. All that I have already said about fly fishing holds good, except that you can go down to a 15-foot rod happily, and perhaps go a little smaller in the size of fly.

## Access

### Lower Tay
Perth Town Water can be fished on a reasonably priced permit from the Director of Finance, District Council Chambers, High Street, Perth.

Access to beats on the lower river is strictly limited and hard to come by. Most of it is handled by various agents, who should be able to provide details.

Tay Salmon Fisheries Co Ltd
Leonard Bank
Perth
*Telephone* 0738 26604

Ballathie Estates Office
Balmains
Stanley
Perthshire
*Telephone* 073 882 250

Bell Ingram
Durn
Isla Road
Perth
*Telephone* 0738 21121

Finlayson Hughes
29 Barrossa Place
Perth
*Telephone* 0738 30926

Scone Estate Office
Scone Palace
by Perth
*Telephone* 0738 52308

Taymount Fishings
Taymount House
Stanley
Perthshire
*Telephone* 0738 828203


*Middle Tay*
Again access is hard to come by, certainly at the peak times of the season. Moving in an upstream direction, the following are worth contacting:

Estate Office
Glendelvine
Perthshire
*Telephone* 073 871 276

Murthly and Strathbraan Estates Office
Douglasfield
Murthly
*Telephone* 073 871 480

Mrs E. Redford (Newtyle beat)
Holmlea
Station Road
Errol
*Telephone* 082 12 312

Dunkeld House Hotel
Dunkeld
*Telephone* 03502 771

Upper Dunkeld Beat:
*Telephone* 03502 8861

M. C. Smith (Dalguise and Farleyer)
Burnside
Dalguise
by Dunkeld
*Telephone* 035 02 593

Savills (Kinnaird Beat)
Chartered Surveyors
Brechin
Angus
*Telephone* 03562 2187

*Upper Tay*
This higher section of the river is more in the classic mould of a
Highland salmon river and, while being in no way small – it is in
fact still big by most standards – it does offer that bit more scope to
the wading fly fisherman.

Logierait and Grandtully:
For details contact Mrs Gray
*Telephone* 079682 230

Sketewan:
Mr John Garbutt
Sketewan Farm
Grandtully
*Telephone* 079682 207

Grandtully Hotel
Grandtully
*Telephone* 08847 207

Edradynate:
For details contact Mrs Campbell
*Telephone* 08874 359

Finlayson Hughes Estate Office
Aberfeldy
*Telephone* 0887 20904

Weem Hotel
*Telephone* 0887 20381

Killiechassies:
The Estate Office
Killiechassies
by Aberfeldy
Perthshire

David Campbell may be able to arrange fishing on certain beats on the Tay, as well as the Lyon:

David Campbell
Keeper's House
Strathtay
*Telephone* 08874 354

And finally, up at the outflow from Loch Tay, fishing is offered both on the river and loch by the Kenmore Hotel (*telephone* 08873 205).

*Loch Tay*
The Kenmore Hotel (*telephone* 08873 205) has fishing on the loch. Other contacts are Croft na Caber Hotel (*telephone* 08873 236), Ardeonaig Hotel (05762 400), Clachaig Hotel (05762 270), Fishers Hotel (05762 285), Dall Lodge Hotel (05672 217) and Loch Tay Highland Lodges (05672 323).

Some of these hotels, naturally enough, reserve their boats for guests staying at the hotel, or certainly give their guests priority. If none of these hotels appeals or can help, boats on Loch Tay are also available from Mrs Hill, Acharn Farm, Killin, Perthshire (*telephone* 05672 317).

# TAY TRIBUTARIES

## TUMMEL

Upper Logierait on the Upper Tay takes in part of the Tummel – its joining with the Tay. Contact Mrs Gray on 079682 230.

Below the famous dam and fish pass with viewing gallery at Pitlochry, the Pitlochry Angling Club has the fishing off the right bank. Applications for permits should best be made in writing to:

> Pitlochry Angling Club
> c/o The Tourist Office
> Atholl Street
> Pitlochry
> Perthshire

Permission to fish the East Haugh Fishings can be sought from Shooting Lines in Edinburgh (*telephone* 031 337 8616).

Loch Faskally, above the dam, is trolled for salmon in the same fashion as Loch Tay.

> The Boat House
> Loch Faskally
> Pitlochry
> Perthshire
> *Telephone* 0796 2919

## LYON

Coshieville Hotel, Coshieville, by Aberfeldy (*telephone* 08873 319), can arrange fishing on a Lyon beat.

Fortingall Hotel, Fortingall, Glen Lon, Perthshire (*telephone* 08873 367), has salmon fishing on various beats on the Lyon.

Finlayson Hughes, Chartered Surveyors, Pitlochry, Perthshire (*telephone* 0796 2512), can arrange fishing on the North Chesthill Estate, as well as on the Meggernie Estate.

## GARRY

For details of salmon fishing on the Garry, Tummel and Tilt, contact:

> Atholl Estates
> Blair Atholl
> Perthshire
> *Telephone* 079681 355

## ERICHT AND ISLA

These two tributaries have a reputation for producing some excellent salmon fishing. Blairgowrie and Rattray Angling Association offers tickets on their stretch of the Ericht through James Crockart & Sons, 26–28 Allan Street, Blairgowrie, Perthshire (*telephone* 0250 2056). The same company should be contacted for details of other Ericht and Isla waters, notably the Craighall beat.

## EARN

It is a mistake to consider the Earn as a tributary of the Tay. The fact is that the Earn joins with the waters of the Tay below the tide and therefore, to all intents and purposes, while being inextricably linked with the Tay, it must be considered a separate river in its own right.

The Earn flows out of Loch Earn, where I learnt to sail between bouts of fishing the river, a good few years ago. It has a considerable catchment area in western Perthshire and three sizeable tributaries but, nevertheless, is best characterised by rather sluggish stretches meandering through the rich farming land for which this part of the country is justifiably famous. It is not all that way, however, and there are streamy stretches from St Fillans, down past Comrie and on to Crieff. Then again at Kinkell there is streamy water, but take caution here for the slabs of red sandstone create some extremely difficult and often downright dangerous wading conditions.

There is a power station with associated compensation flow on the Earn but, nevertheless, it still requires a natural spate in order to show its best, particularly on its lower stretches.

### Season

1 February to 31 October (best February–March and, to a greater extent, August–October).

### Fish and Fishing

Subject to the proviso that spring runs virtually everywhere are not what they used to be, some salmon will be in the Earn on the opening day of the season, and a steady trickle of sport may be enjoyed through to the end of March. But it is in late summer and

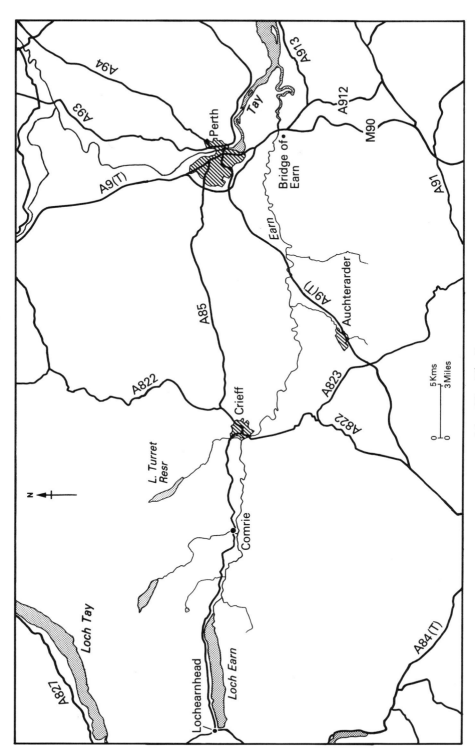

Map 39  *The Earn*

early autumn that salmon fishing comes into its own on the Earn, with sport building up from August through to October.

Because of the character of the Earn it is perhaps understandable that most of its salmon fall to the worm. The prawn is also allowed on certain stretches. The spinner comes second to bait in the league tables and the fly, I am afraid, trails in a poor third. Of all flies, the Stoat's Tail is perhaps the most widely used and, in its smaller sizes tied on tubes, it will double for sea-trout, of which the Earn can have good numbers. The Earn is not a big river and therefore, if you choose to try the fly, a single-handed rod of about 10 feet may see you through, or a 13- or 14-foot double-hander.

## Access

Two permits per day to fish the Hilton beat are available from Bob Sime, Photographers, 57 Methven Street, Perth. This is Perth and District Angling Association water, and, for visitors, it is weekdays only.

Moncrieffe Estate at Bridge of Earn offers permits through Managed Estates, 18 Maxwell Place, Stirling.

Permits are available for the Crieff Angling Club's extensive Earn fishings through local tackle shops. For details contact: P. Dougall, Chief AC Secretary, 2 Duchlage Terrace, Crieff, Perthshire.

The Royal Hotel at Comrie (*telephone* 076 47 200) has a private beat.

# 17 Forth and Lothian

## FORTH

I find myself having to make a confession. Up until fairly recent times I would have sniggered at the suggestion of fishing the Forth for salmon and sea–trout. But there is no sorrow in announcing that I have completely changed my tune. Today I am eager to hear of the what, where and when of Forth fishing, and I am far from alone in regarding it as one of the great success stories of Scottish salmon rivers, comparable almost to what has been achieved on the Tyne in England. In the season of 1988, the Town Water at Stirling alone produced a catch of over 1,000 salmon and grilse. Heady stuff, but it did not come about by accident. We should all give a cheer both

*Carefully does it – a salmon is drawn towards the net*

for the efforts of the Forth Fishery Conservation Trust and a real clamp-down on poachers by the river superintendent and his team of bailiffs.

The Forth is a much longer river than most people seem to realize. Many who cross it on the bridge at Queensferry might be surprised to hear that its source is away over in the west – actually on the eastern slopes of Ben Lomond. Its tributaries are significant. The fact of the matter is that, despite what geographers may say, few salmon seem to view the Ben Lomond option as the choice spawning area. Some continue up the Forth, but the great bulk of running fish turn up into the Teith tributary, and then up its tributary the Leny.

Other significant tributaries of the Forth are the Allan and the Devon. The Allan is now emerging as a particularly good sea-trout fishery, and numbers of grilse are on the increase. The Devon still suffers from pollution in the Tillicoultry area but, nevertheless, enjoys runs of salmon and sea-trout in the later months.

Finally, just to put the jam on the bread and butter of the Forth's success story, here is one river that can boast that its stocks of early-season spring salmon are actually increasing. And these are quality fish. The opening day as far up as Callander on the Teith has produced a 25-pounder. Fish of close to 30 lb have been taken at Stirling in April. And a significant run of grilse builds up through June and July to maintain a fisherman's interest through to the start of the main salmon and sea-trout runs of August through to October.

## Season

1 February to 31 October (best February–April and August–September).

## Access

*Forth*
At Stirling all legal methods are permitted, and it should be added that fishing pressure is quite intense, on the Cruive Dyke Fishings. Day tickets are available from Messrs D. Crockart, Tackle Dealers, King Street, Stirling (*telephone* 0786 73443). Crockart's also sell tickets for the 6 miles of Gartmore Angling Club's water below Gartmore Bridge.

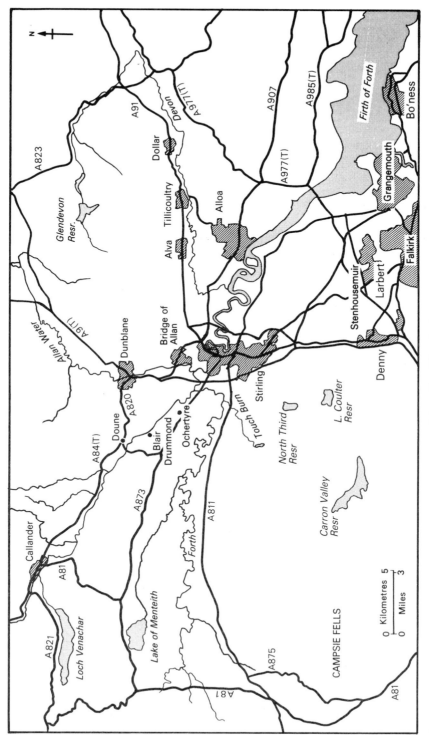

Map 40   The Forth

*The Tributaries*

*Teith*

The Blue Bank Fishings are on the lowest 1½ miles of the Teith, down to where it joins the Forth. Eight rods are available and they may be booked one week in advance from Messrs Crockart (see above). On this stretch the prawn and diving plug are banned.

At Callander, permits for the Burgh Fishing are available from James Bayne, 76 Main Street, Callander (*telephone* 0877 30218).

*Allan*

Some shops in Bridge of Allan, and Crockart's in Stirling (see above), sell tickets for the Allan Angling Association water, which covers most of the river.

*Devon*

The water upstream of Tillicoultry, where the river is cleaner, is covered by the Devon Angling Association tickets, available, yet again, from Crockart's and tackle shops in Alloa.

## THE LOTHIANS

I hope that nobody will be too offended if I say that there are no ᵣeally significant salmon and sea-trout rivers in this area. There are, however, for those who neither wish to fish the many excellent stillwater trout fisheries in the region nor travel south to the Tweed or north to the Forth, one or two minor alternatives. In fact, two is the exact number. They are the Almond and the Esk.

### Season

1 February to 31 October (best September–October for salmon, July–October for sea-trout).

## ALMOND

All legal methods are allowed on the water held by the Cramond Angling Club from Old Cramond Bridge down to the sea. Permits from the post offices at Cramond and Barnton.

## ESK

Fishing on the estuary and river at Musselburgh is handled by the Musselburgh and District Angling Association. Permits from J. Givan, 67 Eskside West, Musselburgh.

# 18 Tweed and its Tributaries

## TWEED

The Wells of Tweed lie at a height of 1,500 feet in the hills north of Moffat on the border between Dumfriesshire and Lanarkshire. After travelling north for a few miles, the confused infant Tweed gets its bearings and turns due east where it picks up the outflows from the Talla and Fruid reservoirs. Six miles farther on, the growing stream is joined by the Biggar Water at the village of Broughton. By this point, the river has already fallen by 900 feet, leaving only 600 feet of fall from Broughton to the sea at Berwick. And so it is from this point that the young Tweed starts its development into a majestic lowland flow of deep dubs and haughs to gladden a fisherman's heart and inspire the nation's finest poets down the centuries.

Above Peebles, the Manor Water and Lyne Water tributaries join Tweed from south and north respectively. More tributaries join before the village of Walkerburn, and 6 miles below Walkerburn is the meeting with the first tributary of real significance, the Ettrick. And the Ettrick has its own tributary, the Yarrow, which can itself produce more than a few salmon each season. The confluence with the Ettrick confluence is regarded as lower limit of the Upper Tweed.

Middle Tweed runs from Ettrick mouth down to Kelso and takes in a string of outstanding salmon beats. Between Ettrick and Kelso, where the Tweed is joined by the Teviot, again a salmon river in its own right, Tweed's waters are swelled principally by the Gala Water and Leader. To me and many others this section represents the very cream of the fishing.

Lower Tweed swells magnificently below the confluence of the Teviot. It sweeps on to the broad coastal plain and can soon be virtually ignored for the purposes of this book on Scottish fisheries. Perhaps a prejudiced Scottish borderer will be able to say that the south bank below Carham fades into the mists of a strange land where uncivilized natives would fish the Sabbath through were it not for the restraining hands of the Tweed Commissioners. And not far after Carham, the whole river disappears into the land where Romans once trod!

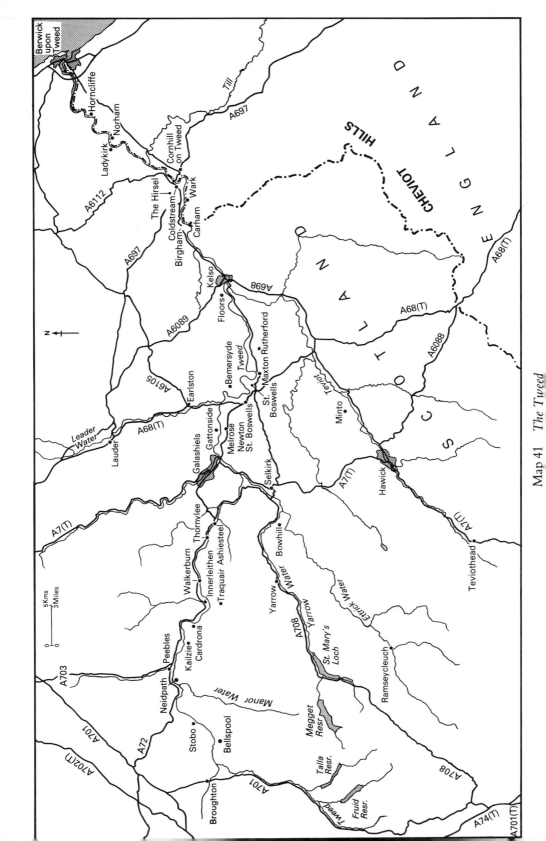

Map 41   The Tweed

## Season

1 February to 30 November.

*Restrictions*
1–14 February: fly only
15 February to 15 September: fly or spinner
16 September to 30 November: fly only

## Fish and Fishing

Tweed is recognized as the greatest of autumn salmon rivers. Sadly, though, its spring runs have been in decline for many years. Beats below Kelso do still have their moments of early-season glory, but they are as nothing to the old days. This spring fishing continues from the opening day of the season through to May. Until the water has warmed, the action stays below the Cauld at Kelso.

Spring fish from Tweed are seldom large. They are typified as game little fish of about 8–10 lb. Those that return in the summer, by comparison, given summer spates to bring them in, are, surprisingly perhaps, a good deal bigger. They are accompanied by grilse weighing down to a couple of pounds.

Once again with the proviso of spates to create suitable water levels to encourage running fish, sport may start to pick up in August, but it will normally be into September before Tweed fishermen can expect salmon numbers to start building up. The equinoctial gales and rain should ensure that Tweed's autumn salmon fishing gets into full swing. Salmon pour up river in their thousands upon thousands. So long as water levels remain high, they will rush on to the middle and upper river, and into the tributaries, but, should water levels fall, the lower beats may enjoy an unexpected bonanza. The average weight of these autumn fish will be about the 10-lb mark, but 20- and 30-pounders are not too uncommon and, just once in a while, a 40-pounder ends up on the bank.

## Tackle and Techniques

Looking specifically at the autumn fishing, I think it is a common mistake to believe that Tweed fly fishing is all about very fast sinking lines and big, heavy tube flies. Certainly such heavy tackle has its place in Tweed fishing, but it is not nearly so significant as some people would have us imagine, certainly not when you get

*Tackling up on the Bridge Pool of the Tweed at Kelso*

upstream of Kelso. Remember that late August and into September can see us fishing floating line and size 8 and 10 flies more readily associated with high summer, in popular patterns such as Munro Killer, Stoat's Tail, Hairy Mary and Shrimp. As an alternative to doubles and trebles in sizes below 4, you can employ the hooking potential of small tubes and Waddington shanks.

As to lines, unless you are fishing a deep dub, you should not automatically assume that you must get some sort of submariner tactics working in order to tempt fish. Many Tweed salmon are actually taken over fairly shallow depths where there is little need for anything more than a medium sinker or a slow or even intermediate sinking line – just enough to settle itself and the fly down into the current. Of course, if the water is really high a fast sinker may be required to fish some of the heavier water effectively but, as I say, do not make the choice of such a line without due thought and justification.

A word on rods. In regard to the Spey and Tay rivers in particular, I have said that I am a great advocate of Spey casting with floating or sinking lines and long rods. My advice is to use as long a rod as you can comfortably handle. If you feel happiest with a 14-footer, then so be it. Most folk settle on a fairly powerful 15-footer, and I use such a rod a great deal and it is more than adequate for most places, most of the time. But, equally, I know the advantages inherent in rods of greater length. Personally, I find any rod I have tried of more than 17 feet to be unwieldy, but if I was a younger, stronger and fitter man, still playing rugby on Tweedside pitches, I might be tempted by another foot. But, as I say, it is all a matter of personal choice, and I hope that I would be the last to encourage you to fish with a rod that does not give you pleasure. After all, at the end of the day, in our search for casting and fishing efficiency we should not lose sight of the fact that fishing is meant to be fun, and that does not include aching backs, shoulders and arms.

And now to flies. The fact that Tweed is a fly-only river in the back end has certainly concentrated the minds of fly fishermen on the design and pattern of fly.

To give you an example of how seriously Tweed fishermen and their boatmen may take the finer points of fly dressing, I will give you just one example. Most people think of the Black and Yellow as one fairly standardized pattern of fly. On Tweedside, however, I have seen at least four variations. Leaving aside the fact that it might have a black body ribbed with silver or an all-silver body, wings may be mixed, tied in two or four bunches, or the whole fly may be tied in the manner of an all-black tube fly threaded above an all-yellow tube fly. Perhaps my best suggestion is to visit a good tackle shop such as Forrest's in Kelso or Angler's Choice in Melrose, and find out who is catching what, where and when, and on what. They will probably offer you a choice from tubes and Waddingtons in sizes from 1½ to 3 inches and patterns such as the Black and Gold, Black and Yellow, Comet, Whitewing, Tricolour, Willie Gunn, Garry, Yellow and Orange and so on and so forth. Take my advice and take theirs, if you see what I mean. All these flies, incidentally, are for use once the water temperature has fallen below 45°F. Conversely, in autumn, we often find that the colder the water gets the more likely are the salmon to take.

## Access

If you want to give yourself a headache, set out on your own to gain access to decent Tweed fishing. To give you some idea of the demand, people are happily paying £15,000 for five rods to fish a top Tweed beat in the back-end months! Of course, it is far from being that expensive on some beats. But wherever you go you will find that somebody has got there before you and that demand far exceeds supply. Neither do I see any point in putting you and those who would receive your letters to a lot of trouble for nothing.

Far and away the best approach to Tweed beats is through a fishing agent.

James Leeming at Kelso has a finger on the pulse of what is happening on many of the Tweed beats, a number of which he represents, and may be able to offer a cancellation or the alternative of 'off-peak fishing'. Telephone him on 05737 280.

Moving upstream, Ted Hunter (Angler's Choice, Melrose, *telephone* 089 682 3070) will be able to give you advice and a realistic portrait of access to Tweed beats.

Farther upstream and well into the upper river, the Tweed Valley Hotel at Walkerburn (*telephone* 089687 636) can often arrange salmon fishing on various beats for guests.

Also try I. Fraser Sports, Northgate, Peebles (*telephone* 0721 20979), who may be able to offer various beats, and who also sell

*Covering the far bank of the Tweed, near Melrose*

tickets for the quite extensive Peebleshire Salmon Fishing Association's water.

## TWEED TRIBUTARIES

Tributaries of the Tweed enjoy the same long season as the main river. They also enjoy the same style of principally back-end sport. Indeed, they can be fished in very much the same way, except, of course, that things are done on a very much more intimate basis. By that I mean that there is not the same need for pushing casting range to the limits. Equally, the size of fly will be that little bit smaller. On a day when Tweed fishermen are using 2½-inch tubes, for example, Teviot may fish well with a 1½-inch, and so on. But the popular patterns of flies remain much the same.

### Access

*Ettrick and Yarrow*

> Buccleuch Estates
> Bowhill
> Selkirk
> *Telephone* 0750 20753

> Ettrickshaws Hotel
> Ettrick
> by Selkirk
> *Telephone* 0750 52229

*Teviot*
Tickets for Kelso Angling Association water on lower river are available from various sources, including the tackle shop, Forrest's, The Square, Kelso (*telephone* 0573 24687).

At Eckford, permits may be available from Mr Graham, Eckford Cottage, Eckford, by Kelso (*telephone* 08355 255).

Jedforest Angling Association tickets from A. Whitecross, 42 Howden Road, Jedburgh.

At Hawick permits are available from Stotharts, 6 High Street, Hawick (*telephone* 0450 72231 or 72334.

*Upper Tweed*
Not quite a tributary but the top of the river. Permission from the Crook Inn, Tweedsmuir (*telephone* 08997 272).

# Index